Should We support the present State of Israel?

(Relationship of Israel and the Church)

Dr. Mohan Z. Mani

BlueRose ONE.com
Stories Matter
NewDelhi • London

BLUEROSE PUBLISHERS
India | U.K.

For permissions requests or inquiries regarding this publication, please contact:

BLUEROSE PUBLISHERS
www.BlueRoseONE.com
info@bluerosepublishers.com
+91 8882 898 898
+4407342408967

ISBN: 978-93-7542-502-1

Cover Design: Deepak
Typesetting: Manisha Rawat

First Edition: March 2026

Should We Support the Present State of Israel? (Relationship of Israel and the Church)

By Dr. Mohan Z. Mani

Contents

Acknowledgments

I gratefully acknowledge the Rev. George Cherian's suggestion last year, regarding the lack of chapter divisions in my former 64-page booklet, "Should Christians support the present State of Israel?..." As per Rev. Cherian's chance remark, that booklet has now been updated, with separate chapters, headings and sub-headings. At that time, Rev. Cherian was the Vicar of the Church of South India, Holy Trinity Cathedral at Kottayam, Kerala. Rev. Cherian also permitted me to sell and distribute copies of the same booklet outside the Cathedral after two consecutive Sunday morning services, on the same day.

I would like to thank my wife, Dr. Anna Mani, and my son, Anand Joseph Mani, for their suggestions, help and great support.

I would also like to thank my elder brother, Sea Captain, Soman Mani for useful suggestions. My brother also arranged a meeting for me on the subject of Israel and Palestine at his Wednesday Night Club meeting in Ernakulam, where even though the audience was small, it was graced by a few intellectuals, including a retired Vice Admiral, a retired Brigadier, and a retired I.I.T. Professor of Civil Engineering. At the end of the session the Professor informed me, that he had received reliable information, that some of the Christian Arabs in Palestine were the actual descendants of the original Church of the Apostles in Jerusalem and Israel !

My brother also helped me to distribute and sell my booklet at the Immanuel Cathedral in Ernakulam last year, after a Sunday morning service, with the kind permission of the vicar, the Rev. John Joseph. Some members of the congregation were keenly interested in purchasing a copy of the booklet.

I would like to thank Dr Shailendra Awale immensely for his great help in analyzing and reviewing the contents of my booklet in two full pages, and in getting this review published in the "Indian Currents," which is a Roman Catholic publication devoted to social causes, and with geo-political overtones. In this way, Dr Awale helped in publicizing the booklet.

Dr Awale is a medical graduate, a Management Specialist and a Policy Analyst, who has been very much involved in social causes. He has helped several organizations connected with the Church of North India, and also the Christian Medical Association of India. He has also been associated with the World Council of Churches.

I am also indebted to my respected teacher in Dermatology, Dr. J.S. Pasricha, the former Professor and Head of the Dermatology Department at the All India Institute of Medical Sciences in New Delhi. Dr. Pasricha was noted as a very eminent clinician, teacher, and a very innovative research worker. He previously emphasized to me the need for an author's repeated editorial corrections and revisions when writing up a book, in order to ensure no mistakes. At that time, Dr. Pasricha had kindly agreed to write the foreword to my book, "Clinical Dermatology through Case Studies," which was published in 2019.

I would like to express my enormous debt and gratitude to my beloved parents (who were the best of parents), Late Dr. (Major) V.M.Mani (Surgeon) and Late Dr. Thankamma Mani (Gynaecologist) of the Uttar Pradesh (UP) Medical Services for their great sacrifice in sending me and my brother to two of the finest boarding schools in UP : Sherwood in Nainital (Principal: Rev. R.C. Llewelyn), and La Martiniere in Lucknow (Principals: Mr. M. Doutre, and later, Col. H.R.H.Daniel), where we were privileged to receive a very liberal education, on European lines, and in a Christian environment. They also sent me for my medical studies to Christian Medical College, Ludhiana, Punjab (a premier missionary institution), where I not only received a sound medical education, but also came to have a good knowledge of the Bible, due to the prevailing Christian atmosphere and warm Christian fellowship there (Director: Dr. Kenneth M. Scott; Principals: Dr. Guy N. Constable, and later, Dr. Lionel. H. Lobo. When I joined CMC as a Dermatology faculty member in May 1976 then Dr. K.N. Nambudripad, an eminent neurosurgeon and Bible teacher and convention speaker, was the Director). I was also greatly privileged to study for my postgraduation in Dermatology at the prestigious All India Institute of Medical Sciences in New Delhi (Director : Dr. V. Ramalingaswamy. Dermatology Faculty Members in order of seniority : Dr. L.K.Bhutani, Dr. J.S. Pasricha, Dr. R.K. Pandhi and Dr. O.P. Singh), where the highest standard of medical practice and research was expected and practised. There, I learned Clinical Dermatology, and the Research Methodology from the most renowned of Professors. I am indeed grateful to God for His grace in granting me all these privileges.

Three of the biggest Christian Publishers and Distributors in India, and even a secular publisher turned down my request for publication or distribution of my book, on the grounds that my book is critical of Israel and of Christian Zionists. I am indeed grateful to the Bluerose Publishers Pvt. Ltd., who are located in Noida, UP, for agreeing to publish this book. I am also grateful for all the help and support given to me by all their Staff and Editorial Team, headed by Madam Arya. Last of all, I would like to return thanks to the Lord for giving me the motivation, opportunity, endurance and courage to complete this book.

Dr. Mohan Z. Mani, December 2025.

Introduction to the Preface, now in December 2025

A) Reason for alteration of the Book Title :

Now, in this new edition in 2025, I have thought fit to slightly alter the title of my former 64-page booklet, *"Should Christians support..."* to: *"Should We support the present State of Israel? ((Relationship of Israel and the Church)."* I have also made minor changes of chapter divisions, along with headings and sub-headings, and a few editorial corrections or additions in square brackets. I have also expanded the original text in some parts, so that along with the Glossary and Maps, the present book is more than double the length of the former booklet.

I have decided to omit the word 'Christian' from the revised book, as this book is not exclusively addressed to Christians. Much less than one-quarter of this book consists of Bible quotations, along with my comments and explanations of the Biblical text. Moreover, people of goodwill of all faiths and religions (or no religion at all), are expected to stand up and refuse to remain silent in the wake of the genocide being committed by Israel in Gaza with impunity for more than a year, and also for all the atrocities committed by Israel on the hapless and beleaguered Palestinians living in Israel proper, and in the West Bank and Gaza for seventy-seven years.

B) Excluded Geo-Political Events are now in Glossary 1 :

Note: I have not included some necessary geo-political information such as the *Intifada* or peaceful march by the Palestinians in December 1987, the declaration of an independent Palestinian State by the Palestine

Liberation Organization (P L O) in November 1988, the Oslo Accord of 1993, and the Abraham Accords of 2020. These are now included in the Glossary 1 at the back of the book.

C) A note about the Glossary 1 and 2 :

A Glossary has also been included, at the back of this book, in this new edition to explain certain theological terms, especially on Eschatology (or the Last Things)—terms such as the Second Coming of Christ, Millennium, and Dispensational Theology (Christian Zionism) in Glossary 2. Besides historical and geo-political events, I have also included some information of important groups such as the Rothschild family of bankers, the PLO, Hamas and Hezbollah, etc. in Glossary 1.

D) A note about Maps:

I have also included, at the back of this new edition free maps of the Middle East and Israel / Palestine from ancient to modern times so that the Reader may better understand the geography of the lands of the Bible referred to in the text, as well as the geographic details of Palestine (In Map 'D' the arrow points to Palestine. In Maps 'A' and 'B' the upper arrow points to Samaria in the north, and the lower arrow points to Jerusalem in the south).

E) Use of Headings and Sub-Headings :

In this book I have broken up the passages in the previous booklet into shorter sections, with the use of frequent headings and sub-headings.

F) A note on Punctuation and Editorial Expansions and Corrections:

For editorial expansions or corrections, I have used square brackets [ ] in the text. For short phrases, I have used single inverted commas such as 'mountains of injustice,' and 'Uncle Sam.' Such phrases are usually seen with double inverted commas, such as "Uncle Sam," but I have avoided it, as double inverted commas have been frequently used in this book for Biblical quotations.

G) Use of inverted commas in Biblical Quotations:

i) In the majority of Biblical passages, where there is no internal quotation in the Biblical text, I have used the standard double inverted commas: e.g. chapter 4 and quotation 1) "For it is by grace you have been saved through faith--" (Eph. 2: 8-10, NIV).

The reference at the end indicates that this is a Biblical quotation. The above reference is from Paul's letter to the Ephesians, chapter 2 and verses 8-10, in the New International Version.

ii) When there is an internal quotation in the Biblical text then I have used single inverted commas for the plain text, and double inverted commas for the internal quotation in order to conform to the double inverted commas found for the internal quotation, e.g. in chapter 4 and the quotation No. 23, it is written, 'John said to the crowds coming out to be baptized by him, "You brood of vipers ! ..." '

H) Versions of English used :

British English has been used for the main text. American English has been used in the text of the two Biblical Versions used here, as the New International Version and the Revised Standard Version are both American Bible Versions, with American-English spellings.

A case in point is the British and American spellings of Judaea and Idumaea. These spellings are British English which is used in the text. In the free Maps, the American shorter spellings of Judea and Idumea have been used. The Reader is informed that these minor variations of spelling are not arbitrary or haphazard, but are there due to the two versions of English used in this book.

N.B. The" New Encyclopaedia Britannica" (Glossary No.18) is spelled with British English, with an 'a' before the 'e,' whereas the " Lexicon Universal Encyclopedia" is spelt without an 'a' as it is an American publication (Bibliography Nos. 19-20).

I) Biblical Versions used in my Quotations:

Kindly refer to the Copyright page for further details.

Preface & Dedication

(As on April 2024, under the title : " Should Christians support..." but now with updates and editorial expansions of the text, in December 2025, with and without square brackets in this revised edition entitled:

" Should We support the present State of Israel? ...")

This booklet was first conceived in November 2023, when I had the 'fire in my bones' due to the indiscriminate bombing of Gaza by Israel for about one month. At that time, I was sharing my views on the Israel-Hamas conflict with a WhatsApp group of my acquaintance, and also received some shared comments from my Readers. After that, I made a careful study of the Bible (without commentaries), and also listened to the You Tube and read relevant details from the Wikipedia to assess the geo-political situation before and after the Arab-Israeli conflict. I have also heard on the You Tube and Wikipedia the history of the early Christian Zionists, followed by the secular Zionists, all of which resulted in the formation of the State of Israel in 1948. I have duly acknowledged all these sources in my Bibliography. I have also cross-checked some of the facts from the New Encyclopaedia Britannica, 15th edition, and updated up till 1997.

Even though I am not able to directly help the beleaguered citizens of Gaza, I could at least share my thoughts in this book. Most of the presentation given in this book is my own, including my interpretation of the Bible in favour of Replacement Theology (as always held by the Church), but also against the Restoration Theology as advocated by the Christian Zionists for the last two hundred years. Even the Twelve Myths about Israel, which I have sought to demolish, are mainly my own thoughts. I have subsequently heard that Ilan Pappe´, the celebrated Jewish historian and critic of Israel, has also emphasized Ten Myths (but different to mine).

I think that I have made some original contribution regarding Israel's claim (or lack of it) to Palestine, the distinction to be made between Judaea and Samaria, as well as some preceding historical factors which could have influenced the Christian Zionist movement. It is quite possible that others could also have made these observations, as they have been gleaned by me from knowledge common to all.

I have in my possession numerous Christian books about Israel and the Second Coming of Christ. Most of these books are favourable to Israel (and are written by Christian Zionists), whereas, some are either neutral or do not mention Israel at all. I have hardly seen or heard about a Christian book which openly mentions about the atrocities being committed by Israel on the Palestinian population under their control, or Israel's lack of justification for holding on to any part of Palestine. Such Christian books, even if available, are not being promoted in India. Accordingly, most Christians in India (at least before 7th October 2023) have had a favourable view of Israel, and a very one-sided, and adverse view of the Palestinian Arabs. They have moreover, not known the historical facts leading to the formation of the State of Israel. Hence, this book !

This book has been several weeks in the writing, and has grown slowly, as fresh thoughts and facts have emerged in a changing, fluid situation. I am still working as a dermatologist, seeing out-patients in a Christian Mission hospital in Kerala. Moreover, my speed of typing is quite slow, and hence the delay. I would like to point out that the total number of casualties of 27,000 mentioned by me was an earlier figure. The latest figure (early April 2024 as released by the Gaza Health Ministry is 32,000 civilians killed and 75,000 wounded (the uncounted bodies beneath the rubble have not been included).

I was privileged to be a medical student in Christian Medical College, Ludhiana, Punjab, from 1966-1971. In those days there was sound evangelical teaching, besides the fact that it was reputed to be a very good medical college. I was able to get a good knowledge of the Bible during my student days there. There were however, some Western visiting preachers and Bible teachers who gave a Christian Zionist interpretation of prophecy (as it was very much in vogue at that time, and they were no doubt sincere Christians). The true facts about the State of Israel versus the Arabs, and the genuine grievances of the Arabs were unknown to them and to me. When Israel took over Jerusalem in June 1967, I myself considered that that was a fulfilment of prophecy. At that time, I had not known any alternative explanations of Bible prophecy, and felt that Israel was the key to prophecy ('soft' Christian Zionism).

In this book, though I have been very critical of the West in general, I am not unaware of the immense contribution of the British (and American) missionaries in evangelism, education and healthcare. Also, the fact that through the universal spread of the English language in the 20th and 21st centuries, God has reversed the curse of Babel (Genesis 11: 7-9). Unlike previously, people belonging to different nations and language groups could understand each other quite well, without going through an interpreter, just by speaking in English. The same applies in India, where English is a *de facto* (but not *de jure*) link language between different linguistic states. So British colonialism was not all bad, but this was not the place to write about the benefits of British colonialism.

The West's ascendancy over the East started imperceptibly in 1492 when Columbus discovered America, and also in 1498 when Vasco da Gama discovered the sea-route to India. Since then, it gradually gained momentum, so that the West has 'ruled' the world for about 250 years now, with the 'sojourners becoming the judges!' (Genesis 19:9). However, this will not continue indefinitely. The Decline of the West, in my opinion, started with the ill-advised invasion of Iraq by America and her allies in 2003, and has accelerated since then. The Ukraine-Russia war starting in February 2022 and the Israel-Hamas war starting in October 2023 have proved to the whole world that the hegemony of the West has been broken forever. So, Israel should soon read the 'writing on the wall,' and speedily make peace with Palestine, and her Arab, and other Muslim neighbours. Otherwise, it may go very badly for Israel, and her very future existence may be at stake.

Many Christians, who are not 'hard-core' Zionists are deeply concerned about the injustice being meted out to the Palestinians, and would readily express their solidarity, if only they knew how! Same, with the ordinary citizens of world Jewry, who are not at all in agreement with Israel's repressive policies towards the Palestinians, or even with the existence of the Nation State of Israel itself.

I would like the long-suffering Palestinian Arabs (Muslim and Christian) to be assured that God is indeed on their side! "The mills of God grind slowly, but they grind very fine." Justice, and a Two-State or One-State solution will be coming very soon. And may God speed the day of its appearance!

I do hope that this book helps to put the record straight, and along with other means helps towards a lasting peace in the Middle East.

THIS BOOK IS DEDICATED TO THE 32,000 + HEROIC AND INNOCENT PALESTINIAN CIVILIANS OF GAZA, AND THOSE JOURNALISTS AND UN AID WORKERS WHO MET AN EARLY AND UNEXPECTED DEATH AT THE HANDS OF THE STATE OF ISRAEL IN 2023-2024.

REST IN PEACE, BRAVE SOULS, ALL OF YOU!

"WILL NOT THE JUDGE OF ALL THE EARTH DO RIGHT?" (GENESIS 18: 25d)

Dr. Mohan Z. Mani. Kottayam, Kerala, India. April 2024.

E-mail: < mohanzmani@gmail.com >

Should We support the present State of Israel? (Relationship of Israel and the Church)

Chapter 1
Introduction

The recent attack by Hamas on the 7th October, 2023 on southern Israel, with the abduction of Israeli hostages, and the killing of 1200 Israeli civilians and soldiers at a Music Festival has once again drawn the world's attention to the miserable plight of the Palestinians, both in the West Bank and in Gaza. These were annexed by Israel in June 1967 and have not been returned till date to the Palestinian Authority, even after 57 years of occupation. [Now in 2025 it is 58 years.]

They have been called Judaea and Samaria by the Israeli PM, Benjamin Netanyahu and his predecessors, but without any shred of international or UN legitimacy. Professor John Mearsheimer, the American geo-political analyst, has stated on You Tube that Gaza is the largest open-air concentration camp in the world, where the Palestinians are living under 'horrible conditions.' The Israeli government has fenced in Gaza on three sides, and denied them free access to the outside world by sea, air or road.

This surprise attack by Hamas had apparently caught the Israeli Government off its guard. In a bid to divert attention from their failure, Israel as usual presented a highly-coloured, fabricated and exaggerated account stating that the Hamas 'terrorists' were guilty of the worst atrocities. To my knowledge, hardly have any of these 'atrocities' been substantiated till date. In fact, some of the Israeli civilians were killed due to the Israeli army's cross fire. Moreover, many of the elderly hostages who were released in November, 2023, contrary to Israeli claims, stated that they had been treated quite well by their captors.

Those who cry foul about the taking of hostages by Hamas should remember that unlike the 240 hostages (figure given by Avi Shlaim) taken by Hamas, Israel has incarcerated thousands of Palestinian men, women and children for many years on the flimsiest of charges, and with no proper trial. The plight of all these illegally-detained Palestinian prisoners has been forgotten or unknown by the outside world, as also the preceding Israeli repression at the Al Aqsa Mosque, along with the proposed Peace Treaty between Saudi Arabia and Israel. It could well be asked as to what other way did Hamas have to draw attention to these facts, and for freedom and justice for all Palestinians, except by these reprisals against Israel?

Great National Heroes

Some Liberators in History who are called great National Heroes by their Countries

It is all very well for Israel, and their great benefactor, the USA, to call these acts as acts of 'terrorism.' But, according to the accepted laws of nations today, and endorsed by the UN, no forceful occupier in any country (in this case, read Israel) has any right to call any act of self-defence on the part of the occupied nation (in this case read Palestine) as an act of terrorism. History is replete with examples of those who rose up against the tyranny of the occupying country, being dubbed not terrorists, but freedom fighters in case they were even only partially successful:

1) William Wallace and Robert Bruce are considered great heroes and liberators by the Scotch because they took on and defeated the much-more powerful English armies in the late 13th century.

2) Shivaji, a Maratha chieftain and warrior, is considered a great hero, especially in the Indian state of Maharashtra, because he harassed the Mughal armies in the Deccan, through guerilla

warfare in the 17th century, in a bid to maintain his independence.

3) George Washington, and his poorly-trained militias took on the might of the seasoned British armies after declaring their Independence in 1776. In case the French Government had not come to the timely aid of the American colonists (now considered heroes), the American Revolution would have most probably petered out, and some or all of the revolutionaries could have been hanged as traitors and terrorists for taking up arms against the reigning British monarch, George III.

4) In the 19th century, Simon Bolivar (now considered a great hero) took up arms against the Spanish Government in a bid to gain independence for parts of South America, notably Venezuela, Ecuador, Colombia, Peru and Bolivia.

Of Hamas, Hezbollah and the Houthis

The so-called militant groups of Hamas, Hezbollah and the Houthis may be called great Heroes later on, as they have fearlessly taken on the neo-colonial Israel and the West.

In the same vein, I do not think that future historians would judge Hamas and other militant organizations and militias such as Hezbollah and the Houthis harshly, once they have achieved their goal of having a separate and fully independent Palestinian State within the pre-1967 borders, existing alongside Israel, and with its capital in East Jerusalem. **This will surely become a reality in the near future, in spite of the best efforts of Israel, America, and some Christian Zionists to prevent it.**

Israel's Right to Palestine?

Does Israel indeed have an unchallenged Biblical and legal right to Palestine?

The question that needs to be considered is as to what is Israel's legal or Biblical right to part or all of Palestine in the 20th and 21st centuries?

In my considered Christian opinion Israel, as a nation, has no legal right at all to any part of Palestine. Those Israeli settlers who bought land from the Palestinians in the late 19th and early 20th centuries have a right to personal possession of land, but not as a nation. They should be under the rightful Palestinian Authority, who are the rightful owners of the land since several centuries.

In case the Balfour Declaration of 1917, and the United Nations Resolution to partition Palestine in 1947 are mentioned as legalities, then the following rejoinders could be made:

i) The Balfour Declaration never promised the Jews a State, but only a Homeland. Moreover, the Declaration itself was colonial, racist, and prejudicial to the original owners of the land--the Palestinian Arabs--as they were never consulted. The concurrence of the Palestinians was never considered at all, in spite of the fact that the Palestinians helped Britain to defeat the Ottomans, because of which Britain was able to obtain the mandate for Palestine from the League of Nations (which was comprised mainly of the colonial powers themselves).

ii) The British had decided belatedly, by their 'White Paper' in 1939 to restrict and then to stop Jewish immigration, and to give the Palestinians their independence within ten years. However, this decision of Britain's was opposed by Jewish terrorist gangs, of which Menachem Begin (a later

Prime Minister of Israel) was a prominent member. They killed 91 people, wounded many others, and purposely destroyed many official documents by blowing up the King David hotel in Jerusalem, in 1946 (this was the headquarters of the British Government in Palestine). Certain Christian Zionist leaders such as John Hagee have later on tried to exonerate Menachem Begin and other militant Jewish leaders for this horrific act and outrage by stating that Begin had sent a warning to the British authorities to evacuate the hotel, but the warning was not taken seriously (pp. 211-212 of Hagee's book, Bibliography No. 21). However, Hagee's excuse and defence do not hold water at all, as this act of militancy could never be justified, even if the intention was to only destroy the records of the Jewish Agency which had been seized by the British, and probably also the land records of the Palestinian landowners (a point not mentioned by Hagee). In case it had been Islamic militants who had committed the same act, then I wonder what would have been the response of the British Government, and Christian Zionists such as Hagee?

iii) Thus, the British were bullied by the Israeli terrorists to hand over the Mandate of Palestine to the newly-formed United Nations. Hagee has specifically mentioned that the explosion at the King David hotel was the 'last straw' in compelling the British to do so : Thus Hagee--an ardent Christian Zionist, by his own admission--has endorsed that this horrific act of terrorism paved the way for the creation of the Jewish State of Israel. Yet it is the same Hagee, who has the temerity to claim that the creation of the State of Israel was in fulfilment of Biblical prophecy! (pp. 11-12 of Hagee's book).

iv) At the end of the Second World War, in 1945 America was one of the two superpowers, and also the prime initiator and founder of the United Nations.

v) The European and American Jews were quite confident that America would act in their favour in Palestine (See the Biltmore Hotel Conference of 1942, in New York, in the Glossary 1, No. 7, at the back of the book).

vi) The UN in 1947 mainly consisted of America and the Western European powers, who were quite sympathetic to Israel due to the problems of anti-semitism, culminating in the recent gruesome Holocaust (which were perpetrated by the Europeans, but not by the Palestinians or other Arabs).

vii) The UN suggested the Partition of Palestine, assigning 56 per cent of the land to the Jews, when even after 25 years of immigration the Jews comprised less than half of the Palestinian population—so even in the land allotment the UN was very unfair to the Palestinians (This could also have been one of the reasons why there was a concerted attack on Israel by the surrounding Arab armies, when Israel declared itself as a Nation on 15th May, 1948).

viii) On 15th May 1948 Israel unilaterally declared itself as a Nation.

ix) The Nakba, or forcible eviction of 750,000 Palestinians which was carried out by the Israelis, should have completely invalidated the claim of Israel to any part of Palestine (even considering that the Balfour Declaration and the UN Resolution for Partition were eminently fair and legal) because this action of Israel's was totally contrary to both decisions.

x) Moreover, the Balfour Declaration clearly stated that the rights of the non-Jewish residents of Palestine should not be violated. This has not been the case, and so in my opinion, Israel no longer has a right to Palestine, even considering the 'fig leaf' of the right conferred on Israel by the colonial powers.

xi) Instead of having only 56 per cent of the land as allowed by an over-sympathetic UN, Israel blatantly holds on to, and controls 100 per cent of Palestine, with impunity, has built a concrete Separation Wall in the West Bank, and has also blockaded Gaza by land, sea and air.

My rejoinder is that if the Americans and Europeans felt so guilty and sympathetic for the Jews of Europe, then why did they not apportion a suitable homeland for the Jewish immigrants in America or Europe, rather than in Palestine?

Chapter 2
The original Land Grant of Palestine for the Twelve Tribes of Israel in 1400 BCE

Going back to the book of Genesis, it is seen that God had promised Abraham (2000 BCE) and his descendants the entire land of Palestine and even more, in chapters 13 and 15, yet, Abraham continued to live in peace with the local inhabitants and never used aggression to acquire land. In fact, Abraham even paid the full market value of the land to buy a burial place near Hebron for his dead wife, Sarah, from the Hittite owner (Genesis 23: 1-20).

In the case of Joshua, and the invading Israelites on the borders of Palestine in 1400 BCE, God ordered for the extermination of the Canaanites (due to their moral degradation and abominable perversions and their custom of child sacrifice, as well as their gross idolatry, all of which would have been a defiling influence for Israel). So, in 1400 BCE the Israelites won the land of Palestine by winning the protracted war, killing the inhabitants, occupying their lands and taking over their houses and possessions. At that time, winning the land by warfare was an accepted international practice. But now in the 20th and 21st centuries CE this is definitely not permissible, as we first had the League of Nations after the First World War in 1918, followed by the UN after the Second World War in 1945, which would never accept such a practice.

God never again repeated a call for genocide after 1400 BCE, except for a brief time in 1050 BCE when God commanded King Saul to destroy Amalek in the First book of Samuel chapter 15 (the Amalekite tribe was descended from Esau's grandson—Gen. 36: 12—Esau was Jacob's own brother). God was provoked by what Amalek had done to Israel under Moses, when instead of helping Israel with bread and water in the wilderness they attacked Israel and tried to eliminate them (1400 BCE). Israel had won the ensuing battle with great difficulty (See the story of Aaron and Hur holding up both of Moses' hands to ensure the victory—Exodus 17: 8-16).

If King David and his son, King Solomon, did not carry out any genocide on the remaining Canaanites in the land, then why should Netanyahu and his backers?

We have a good example of God's not permitting an earlier call for genocide to be 'postdated' in that when King Saul tried to exterminate the Gibeonites in 1050 BCE, God sent a famine as a punishment on Israel. In 2 Sam. 21:1 it is written, 'The LORD said "It is on account of Saul and his blood-stained house; it is because he put the Gibeonites to death." '

The Gibeonites had by deception caused Israel to make a solemn treaty of friendship 350 years earlier to the time of Saul, which treaty was still binding in God's sight. The reference is to Joshua 9: 26-27: "So Joshua saved them (the Gibeonites) from the Israelites, and they did not kill them. That day he made the Gibeonites woodcutters and water carriers for the community. And that is what they are to this day." (N.B. The Gibeonites preferred forced labour, or a form of slavery, to extermination. It is to be noted that this Old Testament mandate is not at all a precedent in the present Gospel Age, for any form of slavery now, based on ethnicity, as the earlier apparently harsh mandates have long since been abrogated).

It is also to be noted that Saul's successor, King David, did not carry out any genocide against any of the descendants of the Canaanites in the land of Israel, as he did not have any divine warrant, and most probably such a brutal thought never ever occurred to him, as the Bible is silent on this issue. It is quite clear that the warrant for extermination given by God to Joshua in 1400 BCE did not extend to

David in 1000 BCE. In case this warrant for genocide did apply in David's time also, then would not God have reminded David about it? It is recorded of David that he was obedient to God in all matters, except in the matter of Uriah the Hittite (1 Kings 15:5) There is no mention at all of the divine displeasure because David did not carry out a genocide in his time, based on a command given 400 years earlier.

Fast forward to David's son King Solomon. Solomon also, did not order a genocide on the surviving descendants of the Canaanites who had been devoted to destruction 450 years earlier, but still survived till then. Neither Solomon (nor any subsequent king) received any fresh command from God for genocide. So, Solomon let those people live but subjected them to forced labour. In 2 Chronicles 8: 7-8 it is written: "All the people left from the Hittites, Amorites, Perizzites, Hivites and Jebusites (these people were not Israelites) that is, their descendants remaining in the land, whom the Israelites had not destroyed---these Solomon conscripted for his slave labor force, as it is to this day."

So how can Netanyahu (and his promoters, 'the hard-core' Christian Zionists) ever justify a call for genocide on the Palestinians about 3400 years after Joshua, in this the New Testament period (or 'Dispensation of Grace' as dispensationalists call it)? They are all indeed without a shred of Biblical warrant, and without showing any 'grace' at all !

After this instruction in 1050 BCE to King Saul, God has never again ordered a genocide either in the Old or New Testaments, and present-day politicians such as Netanyahu have no right whatsoever to again order a genocide on the Palestinians under the guise of destroying Amalek. It is indeed doubtful if the real descendants of Amalek could be found today, 3050 years after God's having issued this command. This command was never again repeated by

God, and so there is absolutely no divine authority today to carry out any kind of genocide anywhere in the world.

Moreover, there are two Biblical texts that clearly forbid any punitive action against future descendants or generations on account of the sins of their fathers or forefathers : 1) Exodus 20:5b states that God's punishment in extreme cases extends up to the third and the fourth generation (this implies that the cut-off period was to be the third or fourth generation—but no more! According to Netanyahu and some of his hard-core and fanatical Christian Zionist backers the curse on 'Amalek' is still valid a full one hundred and two generations after King Saul---calculating thirty years for one generation, from 1050 BCE, a total of 3050 years till today—and they believe that Netanyahu and his most ungodly team are the agents of divine retribution! We, who are Christ's disciples could truly exclaim, regarding such Christian Zionists: " How are the mighty fallen! " (2 Sam. 1: 19b, RSV).

2) Netanyahu and his army of such subservient and appeasing Christian Zionists are also acting against God's dictate given in Ezekiel 18: 20a-b : " The soul who sins is the one who will die. The son will not share the guilt of the father, nor will the father share the guilt of the son."

WHAT SHOULD THE PUBLIC BELIEVE? GOD'S WORD, OR THE LYING WORDS OF NETANYAHU AND HIS TEAM, INCLUDING SUCH CHRISTIAN ZIONISTS ? IF SUCH PEOPLE EXPECT A PLACE IN HEAVEN, THEN THEY ARE EXPECTING TO RUN AN OBSTACLE RACE, NOT IN CONFORMITY WITH THE WORD OF GOD, BUT AGAINST THE WORD OF GOD—AGAINST THE BIBLE, FROM GENESIS TO REVELATION !

This does not give Netanyahu and his team any right over the Palestinians, as it is against all present international law, and the Israelis are the true interlopers and usurpers of Palestine. The State of Israel has been propped up by the collective West for their neo-colonial

agenda in the Middle East, and to atone for their one thousand years of anti-semitism and the Holocaust. All this, at the expense of the poor Palestinians, who had no hand in any of these.

An Absence of Two Thousand Years

There has been a break of almost 2000 years since the Jews last lived in Palestine (in Judaea and Galilee), but under the Roman government.

Israel has no right to Palestine due to lack of continuous occupation since 70 CE, when the Jews were dispersed to the nations and finally from 135 CE when the Jews were finally exiled under the Roman Emperor Hadrian. If we count from 70 CE to 1948 CE it is almost 1900 years that the Jews have ceased to be a nation in Palestine. If God had granted Palestine as a perpetual, unconditional possession to Israel then He would not have allowed them to be out of the land for 1900 years (Judah from Judaea and Galilee) and Ephraim for 2600 years from Samaria. Israel (the ten northern tribes, whose capital was Samaria) was permanently exiled for idolatry and apostasy in 721 BCE, and Judah and Benjamin (the two southern tribes, whose capital was Jerusalem), were exiled permanently in 70 CE, mainly for their rejection and crucifixion of Christ (see Maps 'A' and 'B). So how does this give the Jews the right to Palestine now?

Biblical Samaria

As far as Biblical Samaria is concerned, it is to be emphasized that even in Christ's time Samaria did not belong to the Jewish nation. Only Judaea and Galilee belonged to the Jews, but under Roman rule. So, Netanyahu has even less right to re-name the West Bank as Samaria. There is no prophecy in the Old or New Testament setting a further time period for Restoration of the Jews, and that the Jews would be re-gathered as a nation after two millennia (thereby making the present

'Return' highly suspect). On the other hand, before the Babylonian captivity, Jeremiah had clearly prophesied that Judah would return in 70 years, which was fulfilled to the letter in 70 years. So how do we know that 1948 was the time period referred to in prophecy, and not an artificially-contrived Restoration by the superpowers for their own ends, and not a definite and volitional act of God? Even if we consider Judah alone (and not include Samaria) we can calculate that Israel retained the land of Judah, as a nation continuously only for 1500 years--from 1400 BCE to 70 CE--but they have been out of the land for 1900 years. That is, the total period of their absence from Palestine is 400 years more than their continual occupation of the land. So how does this give the State of Israel a right to Palestine now, when other people have continuously occupied Palestine for at least 400 years more than the Jews ever had it—in the case of Judaea—and 2000 years longer than Israel had it in the case of Samaria?

The Jews (the tribes of Judah and Benjamin) have no claim at all to Biblical Samaria, which was the province between Judaea in the south, and Galilee in the north, during New Testament times—see the Map 'A' and 'B' at the back of the book.

In fact, the present Jews in Israel belong exclusively to the two southern tribes of Judah and Benjamin. The same applied in Christ's time 2000 years ago, as although a remnant of Judah and Benjamin did come back from Babylon in 539 BCE, the ten northern tribes of Israel have never returned after the Assyrian captivity in 721 BCE, and have been subsequently lost to history (New Encyclopedia Britannica, 15th Edition, 1997, Bibliography No. 18, and Craig S. Keener. IVP Background Commentary, p. 744, Bibliography No. 30).

The chief of the ten northern tribes was Ephraim, which, along with West Manasseh, occupied the area which was later called Samaria, from 1400 BCE till 721 BCE. After the deportation of Ephraim and the other nine tribes, the king of Assyria brought in foreigners to Samaria:

"The king of Assyria brought people from Babylon, Cuthah, Avva, Hamath and Sepharvaim and settled them in the towns of Samaria to replace the Israelites. They took over Samaria and lived in its towns...To this day they persist in their former practices. They neither worship the LORD nor adhere to the decrees and ordinances, the laws and commands that the LORD gave the descendants of Jacob, whom he named Israel (2 Kings 17: 24, 34).

Thus, the ancestors of the present Jews in Israel (who belonged exclusively to the tribes of Judah and Benjamin) have never stayed or owned land in Biblical Samaria (north of Judaea) for even one day.

When the remnant of Judah returned to Palestine from Babylon in 539 BCE, they had the unpleasant surprise to notice that the half-breed Samaritans were occupying Samaria. The Jews occupied only Judaea and Galilee in Christ's time, but they neither had Samaria under their rule nor the Greek-speaking Decapolis on the other side of Jordan (corresponding to the tribes of Gad, Reuben and the half tribe of Manasseh—see Map 'B').There was no question of ethnic cleansing of the Samaritans out from Samaria during the 4-5 centuries after the Return from Babylon, even after Judas Maccabeus, and his successors were victorious over the Greeks of Syria and had re-gained full independence for the Jews after 160 BCE. Judaea remained an independent nation for another 100 years (but under the nominal authority of Syria) till 63 BCE, when Pompey and the Romans arrived in Judaea. During the Roman administration of Palestine before and after Christ, Judaea and Samaria were treated as two separate entities, and to my knowledge only the Jews were exiled from Palestine in 70 CE and 135 CE, but the Samaritans continued to stay on and so would have a much greater right to the land now, as compared to the Jews.

THUS, THE UNBIASED READER CAN JUDGE FOR THEMSELVES WHETHER THE PRESENT STATE OF ISRAEL HAS ANY RIGHT AT ALL (EVEN ALLOWING FOR THE DIVINE PROMISES) TO BIBLICAL SAMARIA, AS IT BELONGED TO THE TRIBES OF EPHRAIM AND WEST MANASSEH AND NOT TO JUDAH.

Some of the Jewish rabbis have stated on You Tube that God's decree of banishment for Israel and Judah was perpetual, and so it is blasphemy to think of a re-gathering of Israel at this time in Palestine. As regards the ten northern tribes of Israel—they were exiled to Assyria in 721 BCE and have been subsequently lost to history. So, God's promise to Abraham and Jacob may not have been literally fulfilled, as these northern tribes have been absent for more than 2700 years.

The Final Re-Gathering of Israel as predicted by the Old Testament prophets could be way off in the future and could be just before, or during the Millennium. It should be accompanied by a moral change in Israel as also predicted, as well as a recognition by Israel of our Lord and Saviour Jesus Christ. It should also be accompanied by due sorrow and contrition, which is not at all the case with the present Zionist Israel. It is indeed sad to see how so many ardent Christians have been carried away by this false narrative of a Restored (unregenerate) Israel--stalwarts such as Rees Howells, Leonard Ravenhill and Derek Prince, to name just a few.

Previous Land Migrations

Some Examples of Previous Mass Migrations, but without any claims of Return of Lands

I would like to state that there have been numerous movements, and migrations of populations (with or without wars) all over Europe and Asia during the last 2000-2500 years, e.g.:

1) **The Gauls (Celtic tribes) presumably from Gaul—the modern-day France (or from South-Central Europe)---settling in Galatia---in Asia Minor early in the 3rd century BCE.** This region, now in modern-day central Turkey was named as such because of the Gauls settling there. St. Paul addressed his letter to the Galatians to the Churches that had been established in that province.

   The distance between central France and central Turkey is about 3000 km by the shortest route. Would the French government today be willing to accept the claims of the Turkish people, now in the area of what was formerly called Galatia, and to permit them to settle in France, based on a bogus claim? Certainly not! Then why permit Israel?

2) **The arrival of the Germanic tribes, the Vandals and the Goths in the Western Roman Empire in the 5th century CE and earlier.** They settled in Spain, North Africa and in Italy. Would the present inhabitants of these countries be readily welcome in Germany, central Europe or Scandinavia, because they migrated from these countries 1600 years ago? (N.B. Though some of these countries are today in the European Union, with free borders, North Africa does not qualify).

3) **The Anglo-Saxon arrival in England after the departure of the Romans, 5th c. CE.** In post-Brexit UK today, with new travel restrictions in place, could people in England with impeccable Anglo-Saxon descent, or the English in Northern and Eastern England with Scandinavian ancestry, argue for re-patriation to Germany or Norway and Denmark respectively? After all, their absence from their lands of origin has been much shorter than the two thousand years exile of the Jews from

Palestine. Then why this special consideration for Israel, without any 'fig leaf' of justice, or any agreement with the local, indigenous Palestinians? Is it not a case of settler colonialism, *par excellence* (Richard Wolff, video in 2025, Bibliography No. 16), brought about by the superpower Britain, who instead of 'civilizing the world' has only created mayhem and chaos wherever they went, including in the Indian sub-continent and parts of Africa, but most notably in the Middle East, which appears to be a 'volcano waiting to erupt.' The Ottomans ruled the whole region, including the Middle East for almost 400 years from the 16th century till the First World War, when they were most unceremoniously ousted by the British, with Arab help. One can well compare those 'tranquil' 400 years--a long period indeed--when Muslims, Christians and Jews all lived harmoniously, and contrast Ottoman Rule with only 26 years of British misrule, under their Mandate from 1922 to 1948 to notice that the whole region has been de-stabilized, and made 'ripe for the picking;' and this has been perpetuated into the 21st century by 'Uncle Sam,' the chief scion of Britain. Thus, it took the British only 26 years to 'mess up' what the Ottomans had built up over 400 years. The Reader can well judge what the impressions of future unbiased historians would be in this regard.

4) **The Viking invasions of England and France in the 9th-11th centuries CE:**

In England, Alfred, the Anglo-Saxon king of Wessex, declared a truce with the Danes (9th century CE), but later on, in the 11th century, the Danish ruler, King Canute, ruled England for about 20 years, before the crown reverted to an Anglo-Saxon monarch, Edward the Confessor (who was living in exile in Normandy prior to becoming king of England). Edward, accordingly greatly favoured the Normans at his court, thereby inadvertently paving the way for Duke William of Normandy's claim to the English throne at Edward's demise (see *infra,* point 5).

In France, the Viking leader, Rollo, compelled the King of France to cede territory in the north of France, which was henceforth called Normandy. The chief Norman ruler was henceforth called the Duke of Normandy, and was nominally under the suzerainty of the King of France. The Normans or 'Northmen' were so called because they came from Norway and Denmark in the north.

5) **The Norman invasion of England in 1066 CE:** After the death of Edward the Confessor in 1066 CE (who died without any heir) Duke William of Normandy (who was the most-renowned warrior of his time in Europe) put forward his claim to the English throne and defeated Harold, the last of the Anglo-Saxon kings at the Battle of Hastings. Henceforth, the English language was replaced by French in the English royal court, law courts and higher education, for the next 300 years, till the Black Death in the mid-14th c. CE. So even at the beginning of the Hundred Years War, in the mid-14th century between England and France, the king, nobles, churchmen and lawyers of both countries spoke the same language--French. It has been asserted that if it had not been for the Black Death, then English would most probably have been wiped out as a language. Due to the Black Death, there was a disproportionate death of the higher classes – the French-speaking nobility, churchmen, lawyers and scholars, due to which England was forced to revert to English, which was the language of the ordinary people, who had to be recruited in large numbers, in order to fill the gap (Video

Channel "The Lost Signal" in 2025, Bibliography No. 15).

6) **The Capture of Constantinople by the Turks in 1453 CE with not only a change of language but also of religion (Greek Orthodox Christianity replaced by Islam).** The Turks went a step further and converted the beautiful cathedral of Hagia Sophia (an architectural marvel, with its immense dome, which was built by the Byzantine Emperor, Justinian in the 6th century CE) into a mosque by adding four minarets. The metropolis was re-named Istanbul, in keeping with its new Muslim character. Hagia Sophia had been made into a museum by the secular rulers of Turkey after the First World War, but under the present autocratic and fundamentalist Muslim ruler, Recep Tayyip Erdogan, it has once more been converted into a mosque.

In none of the above cases is a reasonable claim made for return of land or reparations after a few centuries or millennia. Why should an exception be made for Israel, without any Divine approval, and based on certain promises made to the Patriarchs 4000 years ago in the book of Genesis? **As far as Scripture is concerned even the devil is very adept at quoting or misquoting Scripture as in the case of Christ's second temptation as recorded in Matthew 4: 5-6.**

The main claim to Palestine as a land for the Jews in the 19th-21st centuries by the Christian Zionists and their apologists, rests not on the usual rules of law as understood by nations, but on certain Biblical references in Genesis and the books of certain Old Testament prophets. These Biblical references and prophecies are taken absolutely out of context and with great fanciful deductions by these interpreters, which I shall discuss later. I shall also discuss later, the fact that the entire New Testament has hardly anything to say about a Restored and Re-Gathered Israel in Palestine in clear, unambiguous terms during this present Gospel Age.

Chapter 3
The United Nations and Israel

The bold and conscientious Secretary-General of the UN, Antonio Guterres categorically mentioned that what Hamas did on 7th October, though objectionable, did not occur in a vacuum, and implied that it was in retaliation for 75 years of injustice and ignominy heaped on the Palestinians by Israel. The Israeli representative, true to form shouted at Guterres and asked for his immediate resignation. It is well known that Israel has always been expecting kid-glove support from the international community (including the Arab nations) due to the power and influence of their all-weather supporter, the USA.

The UN General Assembly has passed numerous resolutions towards real justice for the Palestinians. It has repeatedly called upon Israel to vacate the occupied areas of the West Bank, Gaza, and the Golan Heights, and to implement a Two-State solution. Sadly, America has each time most unjustly vetoed the ruling in the Security Council in favour of Israel. Is it any wonder that the common Arabs and other Muslims hate the American government and want to get even with 'Uncle Sam' in all asymmetrical ways imaginable?

It is not so well known that in the initial stages Hamas was supported and aided by Benjamin Netanyahu, who wanted to counter the Palestinian Authority in a bid to avoid a Two-State solution. This solution has always been an anathema to Netanyahu and his hard-line 'Likkud' government, which is eager to gain the whole of Palestine. They want to leave nothing for the dispossessed Palestinians, who (the true sons of the soil) are expected to be refugees in Palestine or in any other land to which they could be herded.

It has also been asserted that since July 2018 Israel has the invidious distinction of being the only avowedly racist country in the UN, as according to the new Israeli law which was promulgated, two million Palestinian citizens in Israel Proper have lost their rights of citizenship (Avi Shlaim). So much so, for John Hagee's statement on p.206 in his book, "In Defense of Israel " (Bibliography No.21) that Israel is the only 'democratic' country in the Middle East! This statement, in spite of the knowledge of the *Nakba* of 1948, and Israel's refusal to vacate the West Bank since 1967 !

After the October 7th attack the retribution by Israel was swift and predictable. The Israeli Air Force in a most brutal and cowardly manner started bombing the chief buildings in Gaza, including hospitals, shelters and other public places, with their time-tested policy called 'mowing the lawn,' and with no discrimination between innocent civilians and Hamas, under the specious reasoning that there are no innocent civilians in Gaza, as everyone is said to be complicit with Hamas. Israel has also claimed, but without offering any proof that Hamas is using human shields everywhere, including in hospitals.

Shortly after Israel's onslaught in Gaza, and after the loss of a few thousands of civilian lives (70 percent women and children) the United Nations asked for an immediate ceasefire but most unhappily for the hapless Gazans, and for the moral conscience of the world at large, America vetoed the resolution, and in addition sent its ace aircraft carrier near Israel in order to deter other countries from attacking Israel. At the UN General Assembly 130 countries voted for an immediate ceasefire, and only 10 countries voted against the motion or abstained, including America, Israel, UK and another 7 small countries. It is indeed deeply painful to consider that for the next four months America (under Zionist influence, both Christian and Jewish) has kept on supplying Israel with all kinds of military aid and money to continue the onslaught. This, even though it was known that Hamas could not be targeted from the air, as they were secure in their deep and winding and inaccessible tunnels, both from the air and also on the ground. Till February 2024 America has helped Israel to continue the alleged genocide in Gaza with at least 27, 000 deaths (70 percent women and children) and 50,000 injured. The total figures could be more due to unaccounted bodies below the rubble. It has been stated that the sustained and heavy bombing by Israel in Gaza over 4-5 months [up to April 2024] is the largest quantity of explosives used anywhere in the world since the end of the Second World War, and equals the two atomic bombs dropped by America over Hiroshima and Nagasaki!

It is also to be noted that Israel could not have continued this war for more than a week without American help. President Joe Biden, unlike previous American Presidents such as Eisenhower and Nixon, seems to be totally under the influence of the Israeli lobby in America, the neocons and the American defence industry. No wonder that even before 7th October Netanyahu had allegedly boasted that he 'owned' the American Congress and Senate.

The Israeli army's ground operations in Gaza have turned out very badly, with Hamas inflicting heavy losses on Israel and giving them a run for their money. Many in the Israeli army are part of the conscripted militia, and they have no courage or motivation to take on the ace guerilla fighters of Hamas, in what they perceive to be a losing battle. Moreover, Israel's present war with Hamas has taken the sheen off the much-vaunted invincibility of the Israeli army, as unlike during the Six-Day War in 1967, Israel has been unable to defeat Hamas (a mere militia) even after four months.

The International Court of Justice and Israel

The ICJ in January 2024 decried the wanton killings in Gaza and ordered Israel to stop, but to no effect

The ICJ's Ruling in January 2024 passing strictures on Israel, and asking Israel to refrain from further wanton killing of civilians has been defied by Israel. [But Israel has not cared for the injunction, and has treated it with impunity even till today, in June 2025. Seventeen months later, about 55,000 civilians have been killed in Gaza, and 125,000 wounded. Gaza is still blockaded, and only a minuscule amount of food, medicines and supplies is allowed into Gaza by the Israeli military authorities, who recklessly fire on the lines of starving people, waiting for food and aid. This is none other than Israel's usual habit of ethnic cleansing, which they have perfected to a fine art. The paradox and anomaly is that even though the Jews, most unfortunately suffered from the most horrendous Holocaust under Nazi Germany, the present leaders of Zionist Israel have almost equalled the Nazis, if not in quantity, then certainly in their intention, brutality, and lack of conscience.]

On January 11th 2024 the International Court of Justice at The Hague gave its verdict that Israel was in the likely process of committing a genocide and that Israel should not cause any further civilian casualties. However, the trigger-happy Israeli government and army continues to act with impunity, and is now bombing the southern-most border at Rafah where they had compelled all the civilians to flee, with fresh mounting casualties [This was in February-March 2024].

The International Criminal Court and Israel

Some months after the ICJ verdict, the International Criminal Court brought Criminal Actions, and issued arrest warrants against Benjamin Netanyahu, his minister of defence, Yoav Gallant, and three Hamas leaders, for their crimes against humanity. Certain countries such as the USA, refused to recognize this warrant, and even invited Netanyahu to address Congress, at which time, almost the whole Congress, (due to the power and pelf of the Israeli lobby) gave numerous standing ovations to Netanyahu (or in other words, they 'bent over backwards' in order to eulogize Netanyahu). [The same Netanyahu, who is leading Israel in its genocide against the Palestinians of Gaza---**How are the mighty fallen**! (2 Sam. 1: 19 b, RSV).]

Israel is an unbelieving, apostate nation

Is it not quite clear that this present Zionist, unbelieving and atheistic Israel could be the Apostate Israel which has two horns like a lamb (that is mimics the People of God of ancient times), but speaks like a dragon (Revelation 13: 11)? That is, Israel is guilty of all the unrighteous deeds that the Bible--both Old and New Testament--warns us against and condemns? Notice that ever since its inception Israel has been guilty of dispossessing the Palestinians from their lands, refusing to return the West Bank to the Palestinians since the last 58 years [in 2025], practising the worst form of Apartheid, and now since October 2023 openly practising a form of genocide in Gaza, with more than 27000 Palestinian civilians already dead (70 per cent women and children), [in March-April 2024] and so repeatedly and flagrantly disobeying the Sixth, Eighth, Ninth and Tenth Commandments of the Decalogue or Ten Commandments (i.e. the specific commandments prohibiting killing, stealing, bearing false witness and coveting their neighbour's property respectively—Exodus chapter 20).

A Call to Action by the Global Community

A Call to Action by an imaginary 'Global Action Committee' but *sans* America, NATO, and Israel

Is it not high time now for the Arab Nations, along with the Global South, backed and supported by Russia and China (both countries now equal in military power to USA) to take on Israel, America and their supporters, and to compel them to abide by the Law of Nations (which 'Uncle Sam' and his minions are always admonishing other nations to observe, but hypocritically refuse to observe themselves). They should force a Two-State solution on Israel to permanently solve the Palestine problem. Israel should be compelled to revert to its pre-1967 borders, and the illegal Israeli settlers (who have broken international law) should be evicted from the West Bank, Gaza and East Jerusalem without any compensation at all. In addition, Israel, America and Britain should be compelled to pay full compensation to the Palestinians for all the horrendous injustice perpetrated by them against the Palestinians over the last one hundred years, with impunity (cf. the huge compensation paid by West Germany to Israel as reparations for the Holocaust). And last, but not least, a united, firm and strong stand should be taken by the historic Churches all over the World against Christian Zionism (especially in the Global South, where the influence of the Jewish financiers is much less apparent) by correctly, openly and forcefully interpreting the Biblical Doctrine of Christ's Second Coming. **But the million dollar question is "WHO WILL BELL THE CAT ?"**

Chapter 4
Replacement or Restoration?

The Church has replaced Israel--Thirty New Testament Quotations in Confirmation

The Conflict between Replacement / Succession / Enlargement Theology (held by the Church for almost 2000 years) and Restoration Theology (held by Christian Zionists since the early 19th century--last 200 years only)

Ever since its inception, the Church has always held to the simple Gospel of the necessity for full faith in Jesus Christ for salvation. The following New Testament quotations make the Church's position clear that there is only one way of salvation, and the dividing wall between the Jew and Gentile has been irretrievably broken down by the sacrifice of Jesus Christ on the cross.

Because of this, the Jew would cease to hold a special status under the New Dispensation (and Covenant) but must come to faith in Christ in order to be saved. So, there is no point in dividing up the Gospel faith and insisting that besides our faith in Christ we should also consider the unconverted Jew, and the so-called Restoration of unregenerate Israel with special favour, in order to receive God's blessings.

New Testament Quotations to show that after the First Coming of Christ, the Christian Church has succeeded Israel, and has Inherited the Promises God made to the Patriarchs – Abraham, Isaac and Jacob

Thirty New Testament Quotations are now being given from the New International Version (NIV), which clearly suggest that we, the Church have replaced Israel as God's people, and that we should neither revert to the Old Covenant, nor try to mix the New Covenant with the Old

Covenant as desired by Christian Zionism (a phenomenon and heresy of the last two centuries only):

1) Ephesians 2: 8-10 :

"For it is by grace you have been saved, through faith-and this not from yourselves, it is the gift of God—not by works, so that no one can boast. For we are God's workmanship, created in Christ Jesus to do good works, which God prepared in advance for us to do."

2) Ephesians 2: 14-15:

"For he himself is our peace, who has made the two one and has destroyed the barrier, the dividing wall of hostility, by abolishing in his flesh the law with its commandments and regulations. His purpose was to create in himself one new man out of the two, thus making peace, ... "

3) Ephesians 2: 18 :

"For through him we both have access to the Father by one Spirit. "

4) Colossians 3:11:

"Here there is no Greek or Jew, circumcised or uncircumcised, barbarian, Scythian, slave or free, but Christ is all, and is in all."

5) Matthew 27 : 50-51a:

"And when Jesus had cried out again in a loud voice, he gave up his spirit. At that moment the curtain of the temple was torn in two from top to bottom. "

Comment: This verse clearly reveals that the old Jewish Dispensation of blood sacrifices in the Temple was over for all time, and the New Dispensation of the Holy Spirit was about to commence.

6) John 4: 23-24 :

This was elaborated by our Lord to the Samaritan woman, "Yet a time is coming and has now come when the true worshipers will worship the Father in spirit and truth, for they are the kind of worshipers the Father seeks. God is spirit, and his worshipers must worship in spirit and in truth."

Comment: If the above is true as it must be, as all of Christ's words and his apostles' words are true, then **how can Dispensational teachers such as Scofield and others believe in and look forward to a new Jewish Temple and the restoration of animal sacrifices as approved by God, 2000 years after the all-sufficient and enduring sacrifice of Christ on Calvary? Is this not a contradiction to the pure and simple Gospel of Jesus Christ, and a great heresy?**

I am convinced that if the Apostle Paul were here today, he would have denounced the Christian Zionists with as much fervour and passion as he had denounced those Judaizers who insisted on circumcision in addition to the Gospel of simple faith in Christ. In Galatians 1: 8 Paul has said, "But even if we or an angel from heaven should preach a gospel other than the one we preached to you, let him be eternally condemned! "

I just cannot understand why loyalty to an unregenerate and murderous Zionist Israel is enjoined on other Christians by the advocates of Christian Zionism within the Churches all over the world, but especially in USA and the UK? **Is there to be one Bible, with all its moral obligations for Christians and the world, and quite another Bible, without a God who loves righteousness and justice, and without any morality at all, and with Christ's Sermon on the Mount turned upside-down for the convenience of Zionist Israel, as well as of the powerful and super-rich Israeli lobby in America?** I am not at all against ordinary peace-loving Jews, scattered all over the world, but mainly dwelling in western nations at present, who are quiet and non-aggressive and tolerant. However, Zionist Israel is just the opposite. Their God is not the God of Abraham, but their god is Mars, the Roman god of War (who was disowned and discredited by the Romans themselves once they became Christians). We must not fail to remember that the early Christians were fiercely persecuted by the Roman government mainly on the charge of Atheism, as those Christians renounced their belief in the Roman pantheon of gods, including Mars, as soon as they converted to Christianity. **The unprejudiced Reader of this book can judge for themselves whether my attitude constitutes true anti-semitism or not? To my mind, anti-semitism means targeting of Jews just because of their race, which is not the case here. Christians ought to pray for the salvation of the Jews, as well as of all other people.**

7) Hebrews 1: 1-2 :

"In the past God spoke to our forefathers through the prophets at many times and in various ways, but in these last days he has spoken to us by his Son, whom he appointed heir of all things, and through whom he made the universe."

8) Hebrews 3: 1-3:

"Therefore, holy brothers, who share in the heavenly calling, fix your thoughts on Jesus, the apostle and high priest whom we confess. He was faithful to the one who appointed him, just as Moses was faithful in all God's house. Jesus has been found worthy of greater honor than Moses, just as the builder of a house has greater honor than the house itself."

9) Hebrews 7:11 :

"If perfection could have been attained through the Levitical priesthood (for on the basis of it the law was given to the people), why was there still need for another priest to come—one in the order of Melchizedek, not in the order of Aaron?"

10) Hebrews 7: 26-28:

"Such a high priest meets our need—one who is holy, blameless, pure, set apart from sinners, exalted above the heavens. Unlike the other high priests, he does not need to offer sacrifices day after day, first for his own sins and then for the sins of the people. He sacrificed for their sins once for all when he offered himself. For the law appoints as high priests men who are weak; but the oath, which came after the law, appointed the Son who has been made perfect forever."

11) Hebrews 8:6 :

"But the ministry Jesus has received is as superior to theirs as the covenant of which he is the mediator is superior to the old one, and it is founded on better promises."

12) Hebrews 10: 8-10 :

'First he said, "Sacrifices and offerings, burnt offerings and sin offerings you did not desire, nor were you pleased with them" (although the law required them to be made). Then he said, "Here I am, I have come to do your will." He sets aside the first to establish the second. And by that will we have been made holy through the sacrifice of the body of Jesus Christ once for all.'

13) Hebrews 11 : 39-40 :

"These were all commended for their faith, yet none of them received what had been promised. God had planned something better for us so that only together with us would they be made perfect."

14) 1 Peter 1 : 10-12a :

"Concerning this salvation, the prophets who spoke of the grace that was to come to you, searched intently and with the greatest care, trying to find out the time and circumstances to which the Spirit of Christ in them was pointing when he predicted the sufferings of Christ and the glories that would follow. It was revealed to them that they were not serving themselves but you, ..."

Comment: Peter's First letter, which was written to both Jewish and Gentile believers of the Churches in Asia Minor (present-day Turkey) clearly indicates that the prophets wrote for the Christian Dispensation of this Gospel age, and not for either the unbelieving Jews or an unbelieving National Israel.

So, Peter has endorsed the fact that the Church has replaced Israel in the divine economy for receiving the blessings. So, it is not the so-called Replacement Theology that is wrong and unbiblical, but the Restoration Theology of the Christian Zionists that is erroneous.

15) Galatians 4: 24-26 :

"These things may be taken figuratively, for the women represent two covenants. One covenant is from Mount Sinai and bears children who are to be slaves: This is Hagar. Now Hagar stands for Mount Sinai in Arabia and corresponds to the present city of Jerusalem, because she is in slavery with her children. But the Jerusalem that is above is free, and she is our mother."

16) Galatians 5 : 1-2 :

"It is for freedom that Christ has set us free. Stand firm, then, and do not let yourselves be burdened again by a yoke of slavery. Mark my words! I, Paul, tell you that if you let yourselves be circumcised, Christ will be of no value to you at all. "

Note: We can easily substitute the Christian Zionist doctrine of the Restoration Theology *in lieu* of Circumcision in the above verses, as both are a substitute for the True Gospel. At that time they were referred to as the Circumcision Party or Judaizers, but now they can be called the Restoration Party or Zionist Appeasers (cf. The British Prime Minister, Neville Chamberlain and the Nazi appeasers, who appeased Adolf Hitler in 1938, by the Munich Agreement, and brought on the Second World War in 1939, while Britain and France were in an unprepared state; even so, these Zionist Appeasers would like to have a continuing cycle of violence in the Middle East, and would not mind bringing on the Third World War, by continuing to lend impunity to Israel in its murderous designs).

17) Galatians 5: 5-6 :

"But by faith we eagerly await through the Spirit the righteousness for which we hope. For in Christ Jesus neither circumcision nor uncircumcision has any value. The only thing that counts is faith expressing itself through love. "

Note : Here it is clearly stated that physical descent and an external rite such as circumcision are of no value at all in this Gospel Age, if they are not accompanied by the spiritual realities such as faith and love. These values have been totally absent from the nation of Israel since its inception in 1948, and are probably also absent from the present-day Christian Zionists, who are following and endorsing the neo-colonial agendas of the American and British governments, under a pseudo-religious garb.

18) Galatians 6 : 14-16:

"May I never boast except in the cross of our Lord Jesus Christ, through which the world has been crucified to me, and I to the world. Neither circumcision nor uncircumcision means anything; what counts is a new creation. Peace and mercy to all who follow this rule, even to the Israel of God."

Note : In these verses, addressed by Paul to the Gentile and Jewish believers (the Church) in Galatia (situated then in Asia Minor, and now in Turkey) Paul is clearly indicating that the Church has replaced unbelieving Israel for receiving God's blessings. Paul has even implied and stated in verse 16 that the Christian Church now constitutes the Israel of God (Full endorsement by the Apostle Paul, of the Replacement theology as always held by the Church since its inception).

19) Galatians 3 : 14:

"He redeemed us in order that the blessing given to Abraham might come to the Gentiles through Christ Jesus, so that by faith we might receive the promise of the Spirit."

Note: This verse clearly shows that God's covenant with Abraham has now been transferred to the believing Gentiles i.e. the Church, and the Zionists (Jewish and Christian) should not argue, as at present, that the Abrahamic covenant still applies to unbelieving Israel (in fact two Christian Zionist theologians, Walvoord, pp. 464-467, and Pentecost, pp. 476-477, Bibliography Nos.22 & 23 respectively, have declared that the Abrahamic covenant for the physical Israel to inherit Palestine would only be fulfilled in the future Millennium).

20) Galatians 3: 28-29 :

"There is neither Jew nor Greek, slave nor free, male nor female, for you are all one in Christ Jesus. If you belong to Christ, then you are Abraham's seed, and heirs according to the promise."

21) Romans 4: 13-14 :

"It was not through law that Abraham and his offspring received the promise that he would be heir of the world, but through the righteousness that comes by faith. For if those who live by law are heirs, faith has no value and the promise is worthless, ..."

Note: This verse clearly shows that the unbelieving, physical descendants of Abraham have no right to claim these promises for themselves, as there should be faith in Christ the Messiah, among both physical and spiritual descendants of Abraham in order to appropriate the promises made to him and his descendants. If this is true, then Zionist Israel has no right at all to Palestine today.

22) Romans 4: 16-17a:

'Therefore, the promise comes by faith, so that it may be by grace and may be guaranteed to all Abraham's offspring— not only to those who are of the law but also to those who are of the faith of Abraham. He is the father of us all. As it is written: "I have made you a father of many nations." '

Note: Is it not abundantly clear that God has already fulfilled all his promises to Abraham regarding giving the land to his descendants, as even on the physical level the Jews are not the only descendants of Abraham, as the Arabs are also his descendants through Ishmael and are present not only in Palestine but also in Iraq and Syria (the ancient Mesopotamia).

23) Luke 3: 7-8 :

Even John the Baptist declared to the crowds who came for baptism that mere physical descent from Abraham was not sufficient for salvation, but that there should also be a spiritual transformation:

'John said to the crowds coming out to be baptized by him, "You brood of vipers! Who warned you to flee from the coming wrath? Produce fruit in keeping with repentance. And do not begin to say to yourselves, 'We have Abraham as our father.' For I tell you that out of these stones God can raise up children for Abraham. " '

Note: If the very stones could be turned into Abraham's offspring by God, then how little does mere physical descent mean to God—2000 years after Abraham in John's time and now a full 4000 years after Abraham's time, when physical descent could have hardly any meaning at all.

24) Matthew 12: 48-50:

When we look at the Gospels to see our Lord's attitude to earthly and family relationships and pride of racial ancestry, then we find that Jesus laid far more emphasis on spiritual relationships rather than physical relationships, as the following two examples will show:

When Jesus' mother and brothers waited outside for an audience: 'He replied to him, "Who is my mother and who are my brothers?" Pointing to his disciples, he said, "Here are my mother and my brothers. For whoever does the will of my Father in heaven is my brother and sister and mother." '

Comment: Physical relationships are important, but the spiritual connexion between Christ (the bridegroom) and the Church (the bride) is far stronger than any physical relationship. This did not mean that Jesus did not care for his mother, but quite to the contrary, while at the Cross, Jesus told his disciple John to look after his mother (John 19: 26-27).

Jesus also declared that children ought to obey the Fifth Commandment and support their parents in their old age (Mt 15: 3-6).

25) Matthew 8 : 10b-12 :

When Jesus was surprised by the very great faith of the Roman centurion, whose servant was paralyzed and in great distress, he replied, "I tell you the truth, I have not found anyone in Israel with such great faith. I say to you that many will come from the east and the west, and will take their places at the feast with Abraham, Isaac and Jacob in the kingdom of heaven. But the subjects of the kingdom will be thrown outside, into the darkness, where there will be weeping and gnashing of teeth."

Note: This shows that the attitude of the heart (e.g. the faith of the centurion) is more important to God than mere physical descent from Abraham. N.B. The unbelieving subjects of the kingdom—the earthly Israelites-will not inherit the kingdom of God, whereas the believing Gentiles (the Church) will inherit all the promises made to Abraham.

26) John 8: 44, 47 :

Jesus castigated the unbelieving Jews in John's Gospel, as follows: "You belong to your father, the devil, and you want to carry out your father's desire. He was a murderer from the beginning, not holding to the truth, for there is no truth in him... He who belongs to God hears what God says. The reason that you do not hear is that you do not belong to God."

Comment: What makes us think that the present Israeli Zionist leaders are any different from those unbelieving Jews who were so strongly rebuked by Jesus 2000 years ago? It is even alleged that a certain Israeli cabinet minister unabashedly proposed dropping an atom bomb on Gaza as the final solution!

Very recently [February-March, 2024] the Security Council again voted for a ceasefire in Gaza and Rafah, but most unfortunately, America has again vetoed it for the third time. At this juncture, not only do the ordinary citizens of all the Muslim and Arab countries hate the American Government, but they are likely to be joined by many citizens not only from the Global South, but also from some of the developed nations and from America itself!

27) Revelation 2: 9 b :

Jesus, in the book of Revelation, while addressing the angel of the Church in Smyrna, has drawn a distinction between true Jews and false Jews, and He has also referred to the local synagogue as a synagogue of Satan: "I know the slander of those who say they are Jews and are not, but are a synagogue of Satan."

Comment : The implication of Christ's teaching is very clear : Individual Jews, the Jewish race and even the Zionist State of Israel should not be viewed on the basis of physical descent alone. There should also be a due appraisal of their moral standards, but most importantly, we should pose this rider : "Have the Jews accepted Christ as their long-awaited Messiah or not?" If not, then their apparent physical descent from the patriarch Abraham does not carry any value at all!

28) Galatians 3 : 16:

' The promises were spoken to Abraham and to his seed. The Scripture does not say "and to seeds," meaning many people, but "and to your seed," meaning one person, who is Christ. '

Note: In this passage, Paul has made it crystal-clear that the promises that God made to Abraham are meant to pass on to his only 'seed' i.e. Christ. The physical descendants of Abraham, viz. the Jews just cannot inherit these promises unless they are 'in Christ.' As the Jewish race, in general, has rejected Christ, these promises could not apply to them. **Christian Zionism is probably one of the greatest heresies that the Church has encountered in the last 2000 years. It is so unfortunate that so many apparently-devout, evangelical Christians have left the 'straight road' of orthodox theology to run after Israel, rather than truly following Christ. They are wandering into the 'By-Path Meadow' leading to Giant Despair's tempting but**

forbidden grounds of Doubting Castle, in John Bunyan's immortal classic, *Pilgrim's Progress.*

29) Galatians 3 : 6-9 :

'Consider Abraham : "He believed God, and it was credited to him as righteousness." Understand, then, that those who believe are children of Abraham. The Scripture foresaw that God would justify the Gentiles by faith, and announced the Gospel in advance to Abraham: "All nations will be blessed through you." So those who have faith are blessed along with Abraham, the man of faith.'

Note: This Scripture clearly teaches that faith and belief are essential in order to inherit the 'Abrahamic promises,' and that the believing Gentiles of all nations have succeeded in inheriting God's blessings, in contrast to the unbelieving physical descendants of Abraham.

So it is quite evident that Darby and his school (an immense army today) insist on viewing this clear teaching of Scripture with theological 'blinkers' on.

30) Galatians 2: 15-16 :

" We who are Jews by birth and not 'Gentile sinners' know that a man is not justified by observing the law, but by faith in Jesus Christ. So we, too, have put our faith in Christ Jesus that we may be justified by faith in Christ and not by observing the law, because by observing the law no one will be justified."

Note: This passage clearly teaches that without faith in Christ even good deeds, and an upright moral life would not earn us a place in heaven. How opposite is the case of political Israel, whose moral standard is today one of the lowest among all the countries of the United Nations, and yet this Israel is embraced by numerous people who claim to be Christians!

The Word of God states in Isaiah 5: 20 : " Woe to those who call evil good and good evil, who put darkness for light and light for darkness, who put bitter for sweet and sweet for bitter. And in 1 John 3:10 "This is how we know who the children of God are and who the children of the devil are: Anyone who does not do what is right is not a child of God; nor is anyone who does not love his brother." Jesus warned us in Matthew 6 : 22-23 : " The eye is the lamp of the body. If your eyes are good, your whole body will be full of light. But if your eyes are bad, your whole body will be full of darkness. If then the light within you is darkness, how great is that darkness! "

The hard-core Christian Zionists should truly introspect whether the above verses apply to them or not ? In encouraging Israel in all its murderous actions are they not complicit with Israel? Are they not calling evil good? Some of them, along with Netanyahu are even justifying genocide in this New Testament period of grace, based on an Old Testament command in 1400 BCE given to Joshua! These Christian Zionists certainly cannot claim to be the children of God as they do not love or care about the poor dispossessed Palestinians (Muslim and Christian) who are indeed our brothers !

The Unavoidable Conclusion is that the Christian Church has Replaced / Succeeded the Old Testament Israel for Inheriting the Divine Promises.

All the above thirty quotations when taken together show that that there is absolutely no need to consider the unregenerate nation of Zionist Israel as a close ally of the Church, which needs to be respected and shown a special consideration by Christians. Paul writing to the Roman Church stated that "As far as the gospel is concerned, they are enemies on your account..." (Rom.11:28a). Thus, Christians should be highly neutral towards World Jewry and the political Israel, with neither a special favour towards them, nor any idea of anti-semitism.

Chapter 5
Eleven Proof Texts of Christian Zionists refuted

I shall now quote the usual proof texts of the Christian Zionists, taken out of context from the Old Testament prophets, and I will show that these could not mean the Restoration of the present State of Israel which was formed in 1948. I shall also show how this was purely an accident of history, fully supported by the superpowers, Britain and USA, mainly for the sake of their neo-colonial, utilitarian and financial agendas. As far as the New Testament is concerned, there is hardly a word said about a Restored Israel either in the Gospels, the Epistles or the book of Revelation. In contrast to this, a very important doctrine such as Christ's Second Coming is taught not only in the Old Testament but is also fully endorsed in numerous passages contained in almost all the books of the New Testament. Why this dichotomy about a Restored Israel, which is being parroted by many Christian prophecy teachers, and a total silence of the New Testament regarding it, which is nearer in time to the supposed Restoration of Israel as compared to the earlier Old Testament?

In general, when we examine these Old Testament prophecies, we can note that parts of them **have already been fulfilled after the Return from the Babylonian Captivity in 539 BCE.** Others refer to a future idyllic time when nature itself will be transformed e.g. " the lion will eat straw like the ox" (Isa. 11: 7c). Other passages pre-suppose a great moral transformation for Israel at the same time as their Return to the land of Palestine (e.g. Ezek. 36: 25 a): "I will sprinkle clean water on you and you will be clean ..."

Comment: As we all know, this moral transformation or acceptance of Jesus as the Messiah has not yet occurred, and so the Prophetic Return can only refer to a future Transition Period, just before, or during the Millennium. Paul has also alluded to this National Repentance in Romans 11, as occurring just before the close of this present age. [I have already pointed out in point No. 19, under chapter 4 that two prominent Christian Zionist theologians, Walvoord and Pentecost, have written that Israel's promised restoration to Palestine would take place during the Millennium. That being so, and the Millennium not having arrived as yet, according to the Futurist interpretation of Christian Zionism, the present Jews are merely interlopers and usurpers of Palestine today!]

Eleven Old Testament Prophecies used as Proof Texts for Restoration by Christian Zionist Authors, duly refuted

I shall now quote some of these Old Testament prophecies and comment on each of them, and show how none of them is a fulfilment for the present Zionist Israel. All quotations are taken from the New International Version of the Holy Bible:

Proof Text No. 1 : Isaiah 43: 5-6 :

"Do not be afraid, for I am with you; I will bring your children from the east

and gather you from the west. I will say to the north, 'Give them up! '

and to the south, 'Do not hold them back.' Bring my sons from afar

and my daughters from the ends of the earth--"

Comment: This passage cannot refer to the present atheistic, Zionist Israel as they are certainly not the sons and daughters of God, as they have not yet believed in

Jesus. Secondly, it is God himself taking the initiative to bring them back, and not an act of political expediency as in the case of the Balfour Declaration. In the case of the Return from Babylon in 539 BCE, the Persian Emperor Cyrus issued the decree under God's direction as mentioned in the book of Isaiah. There were some problems even at that time for the returning Jews at the hand of the Ammonites and Arabs who were living in the land of Palestine, but as the book of Nehemiah tells us, the Jews (unlike now) were not the cause of the quarrel. Thirdly, this prophecy could have been wholly or partially fulfilled in the Return from Babylon, as other expatriate Jews could also have returned to Israel after the Babylonian captivity. The Jews were not only scattered to Babylon, but were also dispersed to other nations as emphasized in the book of Ezekiel: "I dispersed them among the nations, and they were scattered through the countries; ..." (Ez. 36: 19 a). So, it is not correct for Christian Zionists to say that after the First Exile they only returned from the east ((Babylon), and so the return from all parts of the compass means the return of the Jews from all lands in the 20th century, and cannot refer to the Return from Babylon about five centuries before Christ.

Proof Text No. 2 : Isaiah 51: 3, 11 :

"The LORD will surely comfort Zion and will look with compassion on all her ruins;

he will make her deserts like Eden, her wastelands like the garden of the LORD.

Joy and gladness will be found in her, thanksgiving and the sound of singing...

The ransomed of the LORD will return. They will enter Zion with singing;

everlasting joy will crown their heads. Gladness and joy will overtake them, and sorrow and sighing will flee away."

Comment: These verses do not in any way describe the present tumultuous history of Israel either just before its inception in 1948 or during the last 77 years. While it is true that under the technologically-advanced Jewish settlers from Eastern Europe the former desert lands in Palestine have been transformed into fertile fields and orchards (with a lot of financial and other support from outside), and so the former part of verse 3 has been apparently fulfilled; but the latter part of the same verse is anything but fulfilled as there is absolutely no joy or gladness or thanksgiving in Israel, as it is one of the most insecure nations on earth, largely due to her moral degradation and bellicose attitude to her neighbours. Israel strained hard successfully at acquiring illegal nuclear weapons (with or without the connivance of 'Uncle Sam'), but has fought tooth and nail to prevent Iran from acquiring a nuclear bomb, and had even bombed the Iraqi nuclear reactor in 1981.

After 7th October 2023 the Israelis have been forced to evacuate northern Israel, for fear of the Hezbollah militia in Lebanon, and southern Israel because of the Hamas militia in Gaza. These happenings do not betoken a nation which is happy and at peace, but rather a nation filled with insecurity and hatred and a total refusal to live peaceably or equitably with her neighbours.

These verses probably refer to a time just before the Millennium (Rev. 20: 1-6), when great physical changes could be expected on the earth (see Proof text No. 3) and there will be a likely national transformation among the Jews (Rom. 11: 26-27) so that they are spiritually fit to dwell in Palestine. At that time, the number of Palestinian Arabs may be depleted due to natural causes, or even if they are there in full numbers, the transformed Jewish nation would be quite agreeable to live in peaceful co-existence with them.

It is to be remembered that even in Christ's time, when the Jewish nation was neither very spiritual nor transformed, they were compelled to share the land with the half-breed Samaritans whom they despised--cf. i) The parable of the Good Samaritan—Luke ch.10, ii) The woman of Samaria—John ch. 4 and iii) The grateful Samaritan leprosy patient, after he was healed by Christ—Luke ch.17.

I would like to ask that even though, in my opinion, the Jews have no legal or Biblical title to the land of Palestine today, why can they not co-exist peacefully with another race, who originally owned the land?

Verse 11 refers to the returning Jews as the ransomed of the Lord, which cannot apply to the present Israel as they have refused to accept Christ who is the true Passover Lamb of God, cf. "For Christ, our Passover lamb, has been sacrificed. Therefore, let us keep the Festival, not with the old yeast, the yeast of malice and wickedness, but with bread without yeast, the bread of sincerity and truth" (1 Cor. 5: 7b-8).

It is to be noted that the ransomed of the Lord will display a strong family resemblance to their Lord, who is a lover of righteousness and justice (Ps. 33: 5, 97: 2b), but these virtues are absolutely unknown to the present-day Israel.

Just as there is a false church (according to some people) and a true Church, even so there is a false Israel that became a nation in 1948. Christian Zionism which caused it was the greatest religious 'scam' and fraud of the 19th & 20th centuries, and the Balfour Declaration of 1917 was the greatest colonial enterprise of the 20th century, carried out under a quasi-religious garb. The true Israel will only manifest itself in the future when Christ returns and there is a national repentance by Israel, and the recognition of Christ as the Messiah (Rom. 11: 26-27).

Proof Text No. 3 : Isaiah 11: 6a, 11a :

"The wolf will live with the lamb, the leopard will lie down with the goat, ... In that day the LORD will reach out his hand a second time to reclaim the remnant that is left of his people from Assyria, from Lower Egypt, ..."

Comment: This verse clearly shows that God has promised to re-gather Israel only after great changes have occurred in nature almost equal to the Garden of Eden, when even the wild animals will live in harmony with each other—carnivores and herbivores—and as this has not yet happened, we are forced to admit that the present forced migration of the Jews to Palestine was not only a geo-political and neo-colonial blunder, and a move to appease the conscience of the West and of the Christian Zionists for the centuries of European anti-semitism (but at the expense of the unfortunate Palestinian Arabs, who were neither guilty of any Holocaust, nor of any anti-semitism prior to the Balfour Declaration of 1917). This is also a most irreverent method of pre-empting God Himself, by 'helping' God to fulfil His promises to Israel.

Proof Text No. 4 : Jeremiah 23: 7-8 :

"So then, the days are coming," declares the LORD, "when people will no longer say, 'As surely as the LORD lives, who brought the Israelites up out of Egypt,' but they will say, ''As surely as the Lord lives, who brought the descendants of Israel up out of the land of the north and out of all the countries where he had banished them.' Then they will live in their own land."

Comment: Notice how the Return of the Jewish exiles is brought about by God Himself, and could have been partially fulfilled after the Return from the Babylonian captivity in 539 BCE. Even as the First Return was from Egypt, even so, the Second Return would be the Return from Babylon, from 539 BCE onwards. There is no need at all to correlate this prophecy with the Return of the Jews in the 20th century under the colonial British auspices ;

This Return could well be for a future time, when a King will reign wisely as the preceding verses point out:

"The days are coming, "declares the LORD," when I will raise up to David a righteous Branch, a King who will reign wisely and do what is just and right in the land. In his days Judah will be saved and Israel will live in safety. This is the name by which he will be called: The LORD Our Righteousness" (Jer. 23: 5-6).

Comment: This prophecy cannot apply to the present State of Israel as neither a righteous King nor the righteous God is ruling over Israel. Israel is the very anti-thesis of righteousness and justice, as she is one of the most belligerent and selfish nations on earth.

They came as sojourners to Palestine after 1922, and just before and after 1948 they have become the judges (to quote an expression from the book of Genesis—19:9, RSV) when they started to evict Palestinians, wholesale from their own ancestral lands in the *Nakba,* and when they unilaterally declared themselves as a new nation in May 1948. Moreover, Israel has refused to vacate the occupied territories of the West Bank, the Gaza strip and the Golan heights which they seized 58 years ago, unlike other countries in similar circumstances. Israel has also continued to treat the Palestinians to a form of apartheid reminiscent of the former country of South Africa.

God told Israel in the Pentateuch to be kind to the sojourners (outsiders) in the land, as Israel had the same experience of being sojourners in the land of Egypt. The full quotation is as follows:

"He defends the cause of the fatherless and the widow, and loves the alien, giving him food and clothing. And you are to love those who are aliens, for you yourselves were aliens in Egypt" (Deut. 10: 18-19).

The present State of Israel has openly flouted this rule, in that even if the status of the Palestinian (the original inhabitant) is downgraded by Israel to that of a 'sojourner' or 'alien' they are still entitled to a better consideration than what Israel has ever offered them.

Proof Text No. 5 : Jeremiah 31: 7-12 a :

'This is what the LORD says: "Sing with joy for Jacob; shout for the foremost of the nations. Make your praises heard, and say, 'O LORD save your people, the remnant of Israel.' See, I will bring them from the land of the north and gather them from the ends of the earth.

Among them will be the blind and the lame, expectant mothers and women in labor; a great throng will return.

They will come with weeping; they will pray as I bring them back.

I will lead them beside streams of water on a level path where they will not stumble, because I am Israel's father, and Ephraim is my firstborn son.

"Hear the word of the LORD, O nations; proclaim it in distant coastlands:

'He who scattered Israel will gather them and watch over his flock like a shepherd.'

For the LORD will ransom Jacob and redeem them from the hand of those stronger than they. They will come and shout for joy on the heights of Zion; they will rejoice in the bounty of the LORD – "

Comment: In this passage as in earlier ones the situation envisaged is totally different from what the nation State of Israel has experienced during the last 77 years:

Firstly, it is the Lord who takes the initiative in the Return of the exiles, but in Zionist Israel's case the world superpowers and secular and atheistic Zionist Jews collaborated with each other to bring this about.

Secondly, it is said in this passage that they will come with weeping and with prayer, which did not happen during the present Israel's formation.

Thirdly, nothing has been said in this passage about the displacement and forceful eviction of the previous inhabitants of the land (the Palestinians), along with the bloodshed that Israel has been guilty of committing both before and since its inception.

Fourthly, there is no shouting for joy on the heights of Zion, but a great feeling of insecurity due to the most ungodly behaviour of Israel.

Fifthly, this passage states that Ephraim (the chief of the ten lost tribes) will also be brought back. Now this is very interesting, as even during Christ's time Ephraim had not come back to Palestine, but the Jewish population of Israel consisted mainly of Judah and Benjamin, with few exceptions (besides the Levites who were not counted as a tribe, as they were scattered all over Israel).

This leads us to believe that when God does restore Israel, he will also bring back the ten lost tribes, and so this present 'Return' is not a fulfilment of this prophecy,

At present, only about 40 per cent of world Jewry is present in Israel (Wikipedia), and is awaiting the Final Re-Gathering, which God has reserved for His own time in the future (and can well do on His own terms and in His own way, without us to help Him, and without any contradiction to either His justice, or His love for all the people that He has made).

Proof Text No. 6 : Jeremiah 31: 33-34 :

"This is the covenant I will make with the house of Israel after that time," declares the LORD. "I will put my law in their minds and write it on their hearts. I will be their God and they will be my people. No longer will a man teach his neighbor, or a man his brother, saying, 'Know the Lord,' because they will all know me, from the least of them to the greatest" declares the Lord. "For I will forgive their wickedness and will remember their sins no more."

Comment: This passage again pre-supposes a moral transformation in Israel, brought about by God Himself during the Final Return of Israel to the Promised Land, and this moral transformation is singularly lacking in the present Israel, as the whole, wide world knows fully well. It could be reserved for a future time, as is so eloquently argued by Paul in the 11th chapter of Romans, vv. 26-27.

It is to be noted that this entire passage from Jeremiah chapter 31 has been quoted by the Writer to the Hebrew Christians (Heb. 8: 7-13), who emphasized that this is part of the New Covenant, in contrast to the Old Covenant, which was repeatedly broken by Israel, and led to their frequent chastisements, followed by the Babylonian Exile.

Thus, the Writer to the Hebrews has clearly appropriated this passage for the Church, in line with the fact that the New Testament does teach a Replacement Theology.

Proof Text No. 7 : Zephaniah 3: 20 :

"At that time I will gather you; at that time, I will bring you home.

I will give you honor and praise among all the peoples of the earth when I restore your fortune before your very eyes," says the LORD.'

Comment: Zephaniah was a prophet in Judah, during the time of king Josiah, in the mid-7th century BCE, and shortly before the Babylonian captivity.

This prophecy could very well refer to the Return from Babylon, and hence, has already been fulfilled long before Christ's time.

Proof Text No. 8 : Ezekiel 36: 24-28 :

"For I will take you out of the nations; I will gather you from all the countries and bring you back into your own land. I will sprinkle clean water on you and you will be clean; I will cleanse you from all your impurities and from all your idols. I will give you a new heart and put a new spirit in you; I will remove from you your heart of stone and give you a heart of flesh. And I will put my Spirit in you and move you to follow my decrees and be careful to keep my laws. You will live in the land I gave your forefathers; you will be my people, and I will be your God."

Comment: Ezekiel prophesied in Babylon during the Captivity. In this Restoration, it is God Himself who takes the initiative, and as there is a great moral transformation among the Jewish nation taking place at the same time as their Return, this has only been partially accomplished in the First Return from Babylon in 539 BCE and after. This has not at all taken place in this Second most artificially-contrived Return from the Nations after 1922 CE. It is most probably reserved for a future Transition Period just before the Millennium, or during the Millennium itself.

Proof Text No. 9 : Zechariah 8: 3 :

'This is what the LORD says: "I will return to Zion and dwell in Jerusalem. Then Jerusalem will be called The City of Truth, and the mountain of the LORD Almighty will be called The Holy Mountain."

Comment: This promise could have been partly fulfilled during the various stages of the Return from Babylon after 539 BCE as Zechariah prophesied after 520 BCE. This promise could not refer to the present Political and Zionist Israel. Jerusalem is a disputed city. East Jerusalem is not recognized by the UN as part of Israel ; and in all the UN Resolutions so far, Israel has been asked to return East Jerusalem to the Palestinians. God Almighty, the Father of our Lord and Saviour Jesus Christ, certainly does not reside in Jerusalem, as the Jewish race and nation has steadfastly rejected Christ as the promised Messiah.

This verse could figuratively describe the Church, which is the New Jerusalem (cf. Gal. 4: 26), or it could refer to the future Millennium (even though there is no mention anywhere in Revelation ch. 20 of a restored Jewish Nation in Palestine).

Proof Text No. 10 : Zechariah 8: 7 :

'This is what the LORD Almighty says: "I will save my people from the countries of the east and the west. I will bring them back to live in Jerusalem; they will be my people, and I will be faithful and righteous to them as their God. "

Comment: This promise could have been fulfilled in the later stages of the Return from Babylon (after Zechariah's prophesy in 520 BCE). According to Ezekiel's prophecy, uttered during the Babylonian Captivity (and before 539 BCE), the Jews had been scattered to all points of the compass, and so the Return could very well have been from other countries East and West, besides Babylon (cf. Ezek. 36: 18-19).

Proof Text No. 11 : Zechariah 8: 16-17 :

"These are the things you are to do: Speak the truth to each other, and render true and sound judgment in your courts; do not plot evil against your neighbor, and do not love to swear falsely. I hate all this,'' declares the LORD.'

Comment: Zechariah prophesied after 520 BCE in Judaea, after he had returned with the first batch of exiles from the Babylonian captivity.

These prophecies could have been partly fulfilled when some of the Jews (the former inhabitants of the southern tribes of Judah and Benjamin) returned soon afterwards from exile in Babylon.

Comment: In the passage number 11, the Lord expected a very high moral standard of truth and righteousness from the returning Jews even in that Old Testament period. How much higher is the Divine standard in this New Testament period, as evidenced by the Sermon on the Mount! The great tragedy is that the Christian Zionists, due to their grossly-mistaken doctrines are quite content to expect from Zionist Israel a moral standard much lower

than that enjoined even in the Old Testament. In fact, the present moral standard of the Israeli nation is probably one of the lowest among all the countries of the world, regardless of race or religion.

In the book of Proverbs it is written, "Righteousness exalts a nation, but sin is a disgrace to any people" (Prov. 14: 34).

IT CAN WELL BE ASKED AS TO WHICH SIDE OF THE EQUATION DOES ISRAEL STAND, AND WHETHER THE ARGUMENTS OF THE CHRISTIAN ZIONISTS HAVE ANY **BASIS IN REALITY?**

Chapter 6
The Future of Israel as mentioned by Christ, by Paul, by Jeremiah and by Isaiah

1) The Future of Israel as mentioned in the Olivet Discourse of Christ:

a) Luke 21: 20, 23b-24 :

"When you see Jerusalem being surrounded by armies, you will know that its desolation is near...There will be great distress in the land and wrath against this people. They will fall by the sword and will be taken as prisoners to all the nations. Jerusalem will be trampled on by the Gentiles until the times of the Gentiles are fulfilled."

Comment: In these words, Jesus had clearly predicted Titus' destruction of Jerusalem in 70 CE, followed by the dispersion of the Jews all over the world, and the Jewish nation's ceasing to exist. Jesus stated clearly that the Jewish Dispersion would continue until the Times of the Gentiles are fulfilled. I would like to ask the question whether the Times (or dominance) of the Gentiles is over? Certainly not! The Gentile nations such as the USA, Russia and China are the present world superpowers, and Israel would never be able to defend itself without American military aid. So, at present, the Gentile domination (American) over Jerusalem is still paramount.

Some have argued that because Israel conquered East Jerusalem during the Six-Day War in June 1967, the Times of the Gentiles have been fulfilled. However, due to the reasons stated by me, this is not the case. The Times of the Gentiles are apparently not going to end soon, as according to the book of Revelation chapter 11 and verses 1b-2, the outer court of the temple remains with the Gentiles: "Go and measure the temple of God and the

altar, and count the worshipers there. But exclude the outer court; do not measure it, because it has been given to the Gentiles. They will trample on the holy city for 42 months."

b) Matthew 24: 32-34 :

"Now learn this lesson from the fig tree: As soon as its twigs get tender and its leaves come out, you know that summer is near. Even so, when you see all these things, you know that it is near, right at the door. I tell you the truth, this generation will certainly not pass away until all these things have happened."

c) Luke 21: 29-31 :

'He told them this parable: "Look at the fig tree and all the trees. When they sprout leaves, you can see for yourselves and know that summer is near. Even so, when you see these things happening, you know that the kingdom of God is near." '

Comment: As the fig tree is considered as a type for Israel, some have misinterpreted this verse as stating that Christ was referring to the future formation of Israel in 1948 by his reference to the budding of the fig tree. This would be a highly fanciful interpretation as Christ only meant this as an introduction to the fact that when we see these various signs being fulfilled, then we can know that Christ's Return is very near (just as when the fig tree sprouts and puts forth its leaves, then this is a harbinger of summer).

In Luke's Gospel, Christ not only mentioned the fig tree, but also added–all the trees--thereby precluding the fact that this is a cryptic reference to the re-birth of the nation of Israel.

2) Paul's statements about the future of Israel

In his letter to the Romans, chapters 9-11 Paul has elaborated on the Mystery of Israel, as well as God's further plan for Israel:

a) Romans 11: 25 :

"I do not want you to be ignorant of this mystery, brothers, so that you may not be conceited: Israel has experienced a hardening in part until the full number of the Gentiles has come in."

Comment: Can we really say that the full number of the Gentiles has come in? Certainly not! For we know very well that the door for the salvation of the Gentiles is still wide open, and numerous people are being saved from every tribe, nation and language even now. So, the full number of the Gentiles has not yet come in.

However, when in God's time-table, the full number of the Gentiles does come in, then the following will occur :

b) Romans 11: 26-27 :

'And so, all Israel will be saved, as it is written: "The deliverer will come from Zion; he will turn godlessness away from Jacob. And this is my covenant with them when I take away their sins. " '

Comment: This refers to the close of the Age, probably just before the Return of Christ, when a moral transformation occurs among all the Jews, along with Israel's recognition of Christ as the Messiah. At that time, or during the Millennium, the final promises of the Return of the Jews could be fulfilled, as mentioned in the Old Testament prophets, and already quoted above.

c) Romans 11: 28-29 :

"As far as the gospel is concerned, they are enemies on your account; but as far as election is concerned, they are loved on account of the patriarchs, for God's gifts and his call are irrevocable."

This verse clearly explains the genius and great talents of the Jews down the ages in all the sciences and arts, and their apparent financial prosperity, in spite of fierce persecution against them down the ages, especially at the hands of the European Church, and secular powers.

3) Prophecies from Jeremiah and Isaiah about Israel

a) Jeremiah 31: 35-36 :

The following passage from Jeremiah explains Israel's great resilience in remaining as a separate people even when scattered among the nations for more than two millennia, when so many other ancient people groups have simply disappeared from history:

'This is what the LORD says, he who appoints the sun to shine by day, who decrees the moon and stars to shine by night, who stirs up the sea so that its waves roar—the LORD Almighty is his name: "Only if these decrees vanish from my sight," declares the LORD, "will the descendants of Israel cease to be a nation before me."

Comment: Israel, according to God's decree has remained a separate nation even when scattered to all the nations of the world. Israel thus does not need the land of Palestine to fulfil this decree of being one nation, as it has been fulfilled even in exile.

In case we consider that Israel can only be considered as a nation while occupying Palestine, then God's decree and promise of Israel being a nation in perpetuity has certainly not been fulfilled, as Israel has been out of the land of Palestine for almost 2000 years from 70 CE to 1948 CE.

There is a great day coming for Israel in the future, but it is not now, as the Times of the Gentiles have still not

been fulfilled, and Israel **is still in unbelief.** God always has a remnant which will be saved. In Elijah's time, there was a remnant of 7000 faithful Israelites quite unknown to Elijah, but known to God (Rom.11: 4).

b) Jeremiah 31: 37 :

'This is what the LORD says: "Only if the heavens above can be measured and the foundations of the earth below be searched out will I reject all the descendants of Israel because of all they have done," declares the LORD.'

c) Romans 9:27 : (Quotation from Isaiah 10:22)

'Isaiah cries out concerning Israel: " Though the number of the Israelites be like the sand by the sea, only the remnant will be saved."

Thus, God always has His remnant.

Comment: Thus, there will be a remnant in Israel who will not be rejected by the Lord. However, the apostle John has written the following in his First Epistle:

"And this is the testimony: God has given us eternal life, and this life is in his Son. He who has the Son has life; he who does not have the Son of God does not have life" (1 John 5: 11-12).

So, we are forced to admit that the Israeli remnant will turn to Christ and accept Him as their Messiah, in order to be saved and accepted by God.

Chapter 7
The Twelve Myths about Israel Demolished

Myth No. 1: God promised the land of Canaan (Palestine) to Jacob and his descendants forever: "… I am the LORD, the God of your father Abraham and the God of Isaac. I will give you and your descendants the land on which you are lying. Your descendants will be like the dust of the earth, and you will spread out to the west and to the east, to the north and to the south. All peoples on earth will be blessed through you and your offspring" (Gen. 28: 13b-14).

Comment: Most parts of this promise have already been fulfilled in the history of Israel, as they did inherit the land till 70 CE (excluding the 70 years of the Babylonian captivity). In their dispersion, they have spread in all directions to all the countries of the world. All peoples of the world have indeed been greatly blessed through the unique offspring of Jacob, viz. Christ (cf. Galatians 3:16, with Genesis 12:1-3, 7a, and with the fact that Jacob was Abraham's grandson).

However, the promise to the land of Canaan was neither unconditional nor for perpetuity. If it had been so, then Israel would not have been out of the land for about 2000 years. In the book of Deuteronomy, Israel had been warned about the blessing and the curse : "See, I am setting before you today a blessing and a curse—the blessing if you obey the commands of the LORD your God that I am giving you today; the curse if you disobey the commands of the LORD your God and turn from the way that I command you today by following other gods, which you have not known" (Deut. 11: 26-28).

As a consequence of disobedience, the following punishment would be meted out by God:

"Then the LORD will scatter you among all nations, from one end of the earth to the other" (Deut. 28: 64a).

So, the exile and scattering from the land were clearly predicted by Moses.

In the book of Judges, the children of Israel were severely punished by God for their wrongdoings and apostasy (shortly after entering the land in 1400 BCE, and just 400 years after God's promise to Jacob), either through the Canaanites, the Moabites, the Midianites or the Philistines, and God intervened on Israel's behalf only when they repented, and cried out to God to save them.

What makes the Christian Zionists think that God will mollycoddle the present apostate, unregenerate and wicked State of Israel and will not hold them to account 3400 years after they first entered the land, and when there could be some doubt whether all the present Israelites (Jews) are all the true physical descendants of Jacob, unlike the true nation of Israel that existed at the time of the Judges, and was severely judged for their apostasy and other wrongdoings ? (Here, it may be noted that even on a physical level the Palestinian Christians in Israel and the West Bank and Gaza are much more likely to be the direct, physical descendants of Jacob, as they owe their origin to the Apostolic, Jewish Church, which remained in Palestine after the Jewish War, till this day. They have never been out of the land of Palestine. It is much more likely that the European Jews have much less affinity to the stock of Abraham and Jacob even on a physical level, after 2000 years of exile, and intermingling with the Europeans. It is also to be noted that the Jews of European extraction look very much similar to the white, Caucasians of Europe than to any other people of the Middle East. It is to be remembered that Abraham belonged to Ur of the Chaldees, which was situated in modern-day Iraq, and so Abraham and Jacob were very much of Asiatic stock and not of European stock. C.S. Keener, in his commentary of the New

Testament, p. 744 (Bibliography No. 30) has stated that after two thousand years of exile, even the veracity of the two tribes of Judah and Benjamin (which were the only tribes, besides Levi) that existed in Palestine during Christ's time, would not have much relevance today, as a matter of authenticity. It should also be noted by the Reader that the modern State of Israel does not permit any genetic testing in this regard, and hence it would be difficult to prove as to who are the true physical descendants of Abraham, today).

The conditions for re-gathering of the dispersed and scattered Israelites were also set out by Moses, as follows: "... and when you and your children return to the LORD your God and obey him with all your heart and with all your soul according to everything I command you today, then the LORD your God will restore your fortunes and have compassion on you and gather you again from all the nations where he scattered you " (Deut. 30: 2-3).

Comment: Note that the scattering of Israel as well as the re-gathering of Israel are directly brought about by God Himself. God will surely bring about the re-gathering of Israel, but only after a great moral transformation has taken place. As there was no moral transformation of Israel (the Jews) in the 20th century, we are not at all convinced that the present formation of the State of Israel in 1948 is the fulfilment of Biblical prophecy.

Myth No.2: God promised Israel not only all of Palestine, but indeed all the way to the Euphrates river, which has never been realized so far :

Refutation: The passage in question is the following: 'On that day the LORD made a covenant with Abram and said, "To your descendants I give this land, from the river of Egypt to the great river, the Euphrates--" '(Gen. 15 : 18). Note that this promise has already been fulfilled in that Abraham's descendants, including the Arabs (who are descended from Ishmael, another son of Abraham's), are already in possession of Syria and Iraq, thereby fulfiling this promise. Jacob, who was the grandson of Abraham through Isaac, was never promised all this vast land, but only "the land on which you are lying" viz. Palestine. Moreover, Isaac the son of promise to Abraham, and father of Jacob had a second son, his firstborn named Esau, who though cheated of his birthright and the paternal blessing by his brother Jacob, had every right then and now to the land of Edom, which was south of Israel, not only in the Old Testament period, but also at the time of Christ (see the Map 'B' where the land of Edom is shown as Idumea). It should be remembered that the Herods, who ruled Palestine and Idumaea during Christ's time, were Edomites descended from Esau.

So, what right does Israel have to claim more land than what Israel actually possessed at any time in the past, even considering that their present claim is just (which is not so, for the reasons already mentioned by me)?

Those Christian Zionists and Bible teachers who advocate more land for Israel (at the cost of the Arabs, whether in Palestine or elsewhere) are not peacemakers, as enjoined by Jesus in the Beatitudes, but are following the way of Cain, who murdered his brother (1 John 3:12), as they are quite unmoved, on theological grounds, for the horrific bloodshed already perpetrated by Israel since its inception in Palestine before and after 1948. They would not at all mind if Israel were to perpetrate further bloodshed, by seizing more territories in the adjoining countries of Syria, Lebanon and Iraq !

Myth No. 3: It is claimed that the promise of blessing and curse made by God on behalf of Abraham also extends to his physical descendants living now in Israel :

The passage is:

'The LORD had said to Abram, "Leave your country, your people and your father's household and go to the land I will show you.

"I will make you into a great nation and I will bless you; I will make your name great, and you will be a blessing. I will bless those who bless you, and whoever curses you I will curse; and all peoples on earth will be blessed through you" '(Gen. 12: 1-3).

Comment: This blessing and curse applied mainly to Abraham, and to his seed or offspring, i.e. Christ—as corroborated and elaborated in Galatians 3: 16, as follows: 'The promises were spoken to Abraham and to his seed. The Scripture does not say, "and to seeds," meaning many people, but "and to your seed," meaning one person, who is Christ.'

This indicates that these promises applied to Abraham himself, and then to Christ and all who are in Christ, and share the faith of Abraham. In the Old Testament period, these blessings could also have been extended to the godly people and prophets in Israel. Just as these promises did not apply to the disobedient Israelites in the book of Judges (whom God chastised through their enemies) **even so, we should not expect these promises to apply to a certain section of Abraham's recalcitrant descendants (the secular and ungodly Israeli Zionists, who have come about 4000 years after Abraham, and have been indoctrinated to come to Palestine by one of the greatest religious and political frauds and 'scams ' in modern Christian history) who neither share the faith of Abraham, nor have accepted his seed, i.e. Christ as their long-awaited Messiah.**

Abraham is indeed the Father of many nations, first of all, literally through his progeny (his many sons and descendants, besides the Jews, i.e. the Arabs and Edomites), but also figuratively through all the so-called Christian nations and Churches, who acknowledge the Lordship of

Christ, the true seed of Abraham. In the same way, all the peoples of the world have been blessed through Christ **(cf. Galatians 3: 6-9 with Genesis 12 : 3b, 7a). This is certainly a strong point in favour of what the Christian Zionists disparagingly refer to as 'Replacement Theology.'**

Myth No. 4: It is claimed that the following verse applies to Zionist Israel: "--for whoever touches you touches the apple of his eye-- "(Zech. 2: 8c) :

Careful reference to the context shows that this promise of divine protection was meant only for the godly remnant of Judah and Benjamin who lived in Judaea in Zechariah's day—after 520 BCE (or to others with a similar faith and devotion), and cannot in any wise be appropriated by the present unbelieving and ungodly nation of Israel.

Myth No. 5: The Jewish immigrants have transformed the desert into a fruitful land, and so they have a better claim to the land of Palestine than the local Arabs :

Refutation: It is true that the native Arabs did not tend the land as well as the Israeli settlers from Europe in the early 20th century. This was because the Arabs remained backward, and their civilization did not catch up with that of the West. On the other hand, the Israeli settlers had better education, better facilities and much greater financial backing, and initially the full backing of Great Britain, after the Balfour Declaration of 1917.

This argument put forward is as illogical as stating that anyone, who can look after my house and garden better than me, has a better right to my property than me.

In fact, this argument is used by authoritarian governments to forcefully and unjustly take away the land from tribals and other villagers and hand over those lands to industrialists and land developers, and with only a meagre compensation paid to the owners.

The Israeli settlers in Palestine routinely disparage the Palestinian Arabs, referring to them as being sub-human, or similar to animals.

[I have been informed subsequently, that Ilan Pappe´, the celebrated Israeli historian and a vocal critic of Zionist Israel, has debunked this myth. He insists that the land of Palestine was not at all desolate, as made out by Israeli propaganda, but that the land was quite fruitful and fertile when the Palestinians owned the land (Video, Bibliography No. 5). Moreover, Elias Chacour, a Palestinian Christian and churchman, has asserted that the land was well-cultivated, while in the possession of the Palestinian villagers (pp. 79-80, Bibliography No. 24); and his father, who was deprived of his land and orchards, was not at all certain whether the new Jewish owner would look after the fruit trees equally well (p. 79). N.B., I had tried to make a plausible argument for the Palestinians, on the assumption that the Israeli narrative of the Palestinian 'waste land' was correct. I have been very much gratified to learn from the above-mentioned statements that this Israeli propaganda was a sheer fabrication. Elias Chacour has also declared that the slogan formerly used by the Zionists: 'A land without a people (Palestine) for a people without a land (the European Jews)' was an outright fabrication and falsification (p. 80, " We belong to the Land," Bibliography No. 24).]

Myth No.6: The stark contrast between the Jewish settlers and the indigenous Palestinians:

Similarly, a very unfair comparison and contrast is made between the economic prosperity and technological advancement of the Israeli settlers, who are seen in a more positive light versus the poor, deprived and less literate Palestinian Arabs, who are living in ghetto-like conditions and are said to be lethargic and lazy, and quite unable to look after whatever property they do have. **It should be**

remembered that in order to survive at a subsistence level the Palestinian Arabs of the West Bank have to apply to their 'overlord,'-the Israeli authorities--for obtaining work permits, and these permits could be denied, according to the whims of the Israeli authorities. [cf. the period in 1 Samuel, when the Philistines were the oppressors : "Not a blacksmith could be found in the whole land of Israel...So all Israel went down to the Philistines to have their plowshares, mattocks, axes and sickles sharpened...So on the day of the battle not a soldier with Saul and Jonathan had a sword or spear in his hand; only Saul and his son Jonathan had them" (1 Sam. 13: 19a, 20, & 22).The clock has now come round full circle, with Israel being the oppressor, and the Palestinians, the oppressed.]

It is indeed reprehensible, that in the wake of October 7th the Israelis have cancelled all the work permits of the Arabs living in the West Bank and have decided to call in foreign workers from the Global South—**that is, their intention is not only to starve out the Palestinians in Gaza, but also those in the West Bank. The money earned by any country which is willing to send workers to Palestine (in place of the Palestinian workers themselves) can be considered as 'blood money,' as it would have been earned to the further disadvantage of the native Palestinians.**

The analogy between the status of the Israeli settlers and the Palestinians would be as childish and puerile as the following past historical situations reveal:

1. In 1947, if the plight of the average Indian and the average British official in India were to be compared and if important deductions were to be made from it, then an indifferent and partisan observer might have said that as the British were so much more prosperous and looked after their property in India so much better than their Indian counterparts that the British should permanently

stay on in India, and that India should not be granted its independence.

2. What would have been the plight of the Scheduled Castes and Tribes in Independent India, if after centuries and millennia of discrimination and deprivation, they had not been granted reservations by the Indian Constitution?

3. How would the native South Africans have fared if they had not got their independence from White Minority rule, and also been freed from the tyranny of the most reprehensible form of apartheid, which was even sought to be Biblically justified by the Reformed and Calvinistic Churches?

4. How would the Afro-American minority have got some respite if the centuries of injustice meted out to them had not been ameliorated by the Civil Rights movement in the 1960s in USA?

We can confidently affirm from the analogy of an imaginary competitive race between the Israelis and the Palestinians, that the Israelis at the very start of the race are very close to the finishing line, whereas the Palestinians are only at the start of the line, so that no real comparison could be made between the two. Aesop's fable of the tortoise and the hare does not apply here.

The glorious period of Arab cultural superiority during Europe's Dark Ages

Even though the present Israelis (the majority of them of European extraction) are technologically more advanced and civilized as compared to the Palestinian Arabs today, the situation was the other-way-around one thousand years ago. At that time when Europe had descended into the Dark Ages, there was a bright flowering of Arab and Muslim culture, so that about 900 CE, Baghdad, on the Tigris river was the largest and most prosperous city in the world, with Constantinople on the Bosporus (capital of the

Byzantine empire) a close second. At that time, London and Paris were only glorified villages by comparison.

In the tenth and eleventh centuries CE the Arabic universities in Spain were the leading ones in Europe, and were established long before Oxford in England, or the Sorbonne in Paris. Mathematics (including algebra), medicine and astronomy were taught to the Europeans by the Arabs, who were at that time intellectually and culturally far ahead of the Europeans.

The Arabs brought the figures 1-9, and also introduced the zero to Europe, from India, so that these simplified figures (unknown to the ancient world, and to early medieval Europe) are still called the Arabic figures. Many words from the Arabic have come into the European vocabulary, such as algebra, alcohol, zenith and even admiral.

Moreover, during the Crusades starting in 1096 CE, the Europeans gained immensely from Arabic culture and civilization in Palestine, Syria and Egypt, especially regarding medical knowledge.

Gothic architecture commenced in 1135 CE with the renovation of the Basilica Church of St. Denis outside Paris, by Abbe´ Suger. As the First Crusade had predominantly a French contingent, it is open to debate whether even in the evolution of Gothic architecture (the most famous being the Cathedral of Notre Dame in Paris) the Europeans could have been indirectly influenced by the Middle East (even though this is not generally acknowledged by the Europeans, who claim that Gothic architecture evolved from the earlier Romanesque architecture). However, my suggestion regarding the commencement of Gothic architecture shortly after the First Crusade should offer food for thought!

Myth No. 7: Israel was able to come out as the victor on three occasions, in 1948, 1967 and 1973 against the united strength of all the neighbouring Arab nations such as Egypt, Syria and Jordan, and so these victories point to supernatural help received from God :

However, nothing could be further from the truth, as the following points will show:

1. The Arabs were technologically far inferior to the Israelis, were disunited, and the Arab attacks were not properly coordinated, and hence petered out.
2. Each time the Israelis received massive aid in the form of money, materials, and intelligence from the superpower : America, and so it is not at all surprising that Israel won each time.

In case Israel had won each time without any outside aid, then we could have considered that God was indeed on Israel's side (but this is not the case, as I have shown). In this connexion, consider the case of Abraham, who after the defeat of the kings would not accept any gift at all from the king of Sodom, lest he should say that, 'I made Abram rich.' (Gen. 14:23c). So, it is quite clear that when help is also received from man, we just cannot attribute all to God himself (This does not mean that means are not important, and that God does not work through people in some or in many cases).

The American retired colonel, Douglas Macgregor, has stated on You Tube that early in the united Arab war against Israel in 1948, Israel would have been wiped out in case America had not intervened and helped Israel in a massive way. President Harry Truman of America was approached by his advisers and told that in case he decided to send timely aid to Israel, the powerful Jewish financiers in USA would continue to provide an inexhaustible fund to his Democratic party to fight its elections each time. This does have a ring of truth about it as the New Encyclopaedia Britannica, 1997, endorses the fact that Truman did pressurize Britain to allow more Jewish refugees in to Palestine before 1948. [In addition, due to Britain's belated decision in 1939 to publish a 'White Paper' and to restrict and stop further Jewish immigration, in a bid to give independence to the Palestinians later on, the European Jews decided to transfer their allegiance from Britain to America. At the Biltmore Hotel Conference in New York, in 1942, under Jewish pressure, it was decided to support an independent Jewish commonwealth in Palestine, and which was to be largely supported by American political leaders (Lexicon Universal Encyclopedia, 1989, and New Encyclopaedia Britannica, 1997).]

And so, the inordinate influence of the Jewish lobby has continued to influence American politics right till now. Christ told his disciples and the world at large "You cannot serve God and mammon" (Mt. 6: 24 d—RSV). The political elites on Capitol Hill in Washington DC have continued to clearly demonstrate to the whole world that their true preference is for mammon (riches) and not for the God of righteousness and justice (Psalm 33: 5, 97: 2b).

At this time the Israeli lobby in USA consists not only of Jewish financiers, but also of the fundamentalist Christian Zionists. They are quite willing to help Israel (even when it is wilfully committing a genocide), but at the same time to betray Jesus Christ's righteous commands as stated in the Sermon on the Mount. All of them are complicit with the American government in the genocide carried out by Israel in Gaza for the last five months (as of now in mid-March 2024). I do not think that any hard-core Christian Zionist is willing to put themselves in the Palestinians' shoes. I wonder whether any of them would be ever willing to surrender house or land under similar circumstances, or even be willing to endure one-tenth of the hardships suffered by the Palestinians?

Myth No. 8: The blossoming of the Fig tree in Christ's Olivet discourse is prophetic for the formation of Israel in 1948 :

I have already argued against this above, along with my reasons.

Myth No. 9: The Times of the Gentiles ended in June 1967, when Israel captured East Jerusalem from the Arabs :

Here also, I have shown with my reasons why this is not so.

Myth No, 10: The Israelis are basically peace-loving people, but their Arab neighbours will not allow Israel to exist in peace, and would like to drive them into the sea :

I would like to point out that prior to the Balfour Declaration of 1917, there was complete peace and harmony between people and communities not only in Palestine but also in other parts of the Ottoman empire. The Jews constituted a very small minority, but were fully tolerated and were permitted to practise their religion in peace (Avi Shlaim).

The problems started in Palestine after the Balfour Declaration which was made without any consultation with the Palestinian Arabs, who owned the lands. Riots broke out on the part of the Palestinians, who were being evicted from their lands, or faced various inconveniences due to the constant waves of Jewish immigration, which was at first encouraged by the British. The British are said to have suppressed these Arab revolts with great ferocity, and with the help of the Indian army on occasions.

Then in 1948 May, and just before, when Israel declared itself as a Nation State, it evicted 750,000 Palestinians from their homes, and sent them out as refugees (Avi Shlaim). That is also the reason why all the surrounding Arab nations attacked Israel in the First Arab-Israeli war of 1948. **Most unfortunately for them and for the Palestinians, the Arabs were soundly defeated by the Israelis, largely due to massive support from America.**

The deprived Palestinians are constantly trying to achieve their freedom in a Two-State solution, which Israel is quite unwilling to concede. As already stated, the forceful occupier (Israel) cannot dub the occupied Palestinians who fight for their freedom and basic rights as terrorists.

MOST UNFORTUNATELY, ISRAEL HAS BEEN PRACTISING THE WORST FORM OF STATE TERRORISM ON THE PALESTINIANS FOR 77 YEARS, WITH IMPUNITY.

SO LET US NO LONGER BELIEVE THE FALSE NARRATIVE OF ISRAEL AND 'UNCLE SAM' REGARDING ARAB AND PALESTINIAN TERRORISM, WHEN THE ACTUAL TRUTH IS THE OTHER WAY AROUND.

Myth No. 11: Britain lost its title 'Great' due to the British Government's decision to restrict Jewish immigration after 1939 :

It has been wrongly stated by Christian Zionists in their books and speeches that Britain lost its title 'Great' in what was formerly called 'Great Britain,' because Britain did not help the Jewish project in Palestine enough, especially when she started restricting Jewish immigration, after publishing a 'White Paper' in 1939 (All this talk in spite of the gross and unfair favouritism shown to the Jews by the Balfour Declaration and after).

The Christian Zionists are being very naïve when they make this nostalgic statement, because they fail to realize, a) That Britain was economically shattered by two World Wars, and b) Very shortly afterwards, in 1947, she lost India, 'the Jewel in the Crown,' which had given such an unfair advantage to Britain over every other European rival

(It is asserted that in the late 17th century the revenue of the Mughal Emperor, Aurangzeb was 10-20 times greater than the revenue of his contemporary, Louis XIV of France, who was acknowledged to be the 'Sun King' of Europe—the higher and lower figures are given by Indian and European authorities respectively. Aurangzeb's Empire would have been just about five times larger than France, and so even area for area, Mughal India had a much higher GDP than the richest country in Europe. Moreover by 1800 CE, when Britain had gained almost the full control over India, India's share of the entire world GDP was 20-25 per cent. However, by the time Britain was done with India 150 years later, by 1947, India's share of the world GDP became a paltry one to two per cent, leaving India as one of the poorest and most deprived nations in the world). No wonder the former British Prime Minister, Boris Johnson, and others like him, have lamented the loss of the British Empire! **And so, the decline of Britain could easily be explained by these two historical factors. If at all Israel does come in to the equation, in my opinion it is because Britain helped Israel 'too much and not too little' as God is a God of righteousness and justice (Psalm 33: 5, 97: 2b).**

Myth No. 12: God is always on the side of Israel:

This myth is similar to myth No. 7, but it is not the same. In case 'God' is always on the side of the State of Israel, then it is not the God of the Bible, of whom the following is said: "The Lord loves righteousness and justice; the earth is full of his unfailing love" (Psalm 33: 5; 89: 14a). It has already been pointed out earlier from the book of Judges that whenever Israel was disobedient, God did not help them but permitted the enemy to win. So, we should not expect God to help the present State of Israel, which does not even believe in Him!

Chapter 8
The Origins of the Israel-Palestine Conflict, from the beginning

I would say that if the earliest and most significant date were to be given for the origin of the Israel-Palestine conflict, then we should go back more than 200 years to the famous battle of Waterloo in June 1815, with Britain emerging as the unchallenged economic superpower, while retaining her mastery over the seas, and with an inexhaustible treasury due to her conquest and colonization of India.

I shall now be setting out in sequence, the causes, the motives, the religious and geo-political events that preceded and led to this interminable conflict in the Middle East. This Conflict was started and created by Great Britain during the hey-day of her colonial glory, and now after World War 2 is being eagerly fostered and cherished by Britain's chief scion, the USA, in favour of their colonial agenda in the Middle East.

The First Driving Force to the present conflict in the Middle East in general, and Palestine in particular: The Rise of Britain as the Global Superpower in 1815 :

Britain won the Napoleonic War in 1815 (along with her allies : Austria, Prussia and Russia), and went on to become the foremost superpower financially, while also retaining her status as the sole Mistress of the Seas.

The Battle of Waterloo was fought on the 18th June 1815, near Brussels in Belgium. The Allies under the Duke of Wellington (British) and Marshal Blücher (Prussian, or East German) gained a last-moment fluke victory over Napoleon at Waterloo by a sort of coincidence or happenstance, that precipitated Britain to further world conquest (particularly in the countries of the present Global South in Asia and Africa).

Some details of the Battle of Waterloo: Its consequences and possible under-currents:

By the late afternoon of the battle Wellington (who commanded a mixed army of British, Dutch, Belgian and German troops) was on the verge of losing the battle, and uttered the words, "Would to God that night or Blücher would come!" However, Blücher, who had been defeated by Napoleon in the preceding battle of Ligny, but was not annihilated, and hence (unknown to Napoleon) had retreated in good order. He was wounded in the leg, but did not take the advice of his officers, who suggested a total retreat from further action, but insisted on keeping his 'tryst' with Wellington, by joining him at Waterloo. So Blücher forced himself and his army to reach the field of Waterloo, even though "his soldiers grumbled horribly." Blücher reached the battle ground in the nick of time to turn the tide of battle, and to ensure Napoleon's complete defeat.

Just after winning the battle Blücher approached Wellington, apparently without an interpreter, and exclaimed in French, "quelle affaire!" – by which he meant: "What a terrible battle!" They both had to converse in the language of their common foe (as French was the language of European diplomacy at that time) and Wellington did not know German and Blücher knew no English.

The battle of Waterloo might have ended quite differently, as was commonly expected, as Napoleon was the military genius of his age, and neither the British duke nor the German marshal were any match for him. Napoleon's greatest mistake (besides permitting Marshal Ney, the 'bravest of the brave' to launch his useless cavalry charges against Wellington's well-trained army in square formation, strengthened with bayonets), was to have started the battle late due to the rain, and also to have entrusted a large army under Marshal Grouchy to hold off Blücher and to prevent him from joining Wellington. Most unfortunately for Napoleon and the French army, Grouchy neither held off Blücher, nor did he join Napoleon at Waterloo (even though his scouts could hear the roar of the cannons, signalling the fact that the battle had commenced. The soldiers had urged Grouchy to go to Napoleon's immediate aid, but Grouchy refused to do so, citing Napoleon's previous order to hold off Blücher). Napoleon in his memoirs written during his final exile at St. Helena, rightly blamed Grouchy for his defeat at Waterloo.

And thus this last and one of his greatest battles was lost by Napoleon, leading to profound political changes, a reversal of all Napoleon's liberal policies in France and in Western Europe, and a return to the Bourbon monarchy in France. As a consequence, it was Britain which gained the maximum advantage towards further aggrandizement, colonization and world hegemony, from which ill-effects the nations of the Global South in Asia and Africa are still reeling under today, and desperately trying to fend off now in the early 21st century.

Could there have been some hidden motive, such as bribery and a future promised advancement or leniency, which could have influenced Grouchy and other French leaders in their possible act of betrayal? It is not so well known that the Rothschild family of bankers had formerly helped Britain to evade Napoleon's Continental blockade by smuggling manufactured British goods in to Russia and other countries in contravention of Napoleon's Berlin Decree. This open defiance by Russia had led to Napoleon's disastrous invasion of Russia, leading to his overthrow and first exile to Elba in 1814. As the Rothschilds were very active in loaning money to both Britain and France during the entire Napoleonic War, it is quite possible that the Rothschilds could have been indirectly responsible for Napoleon's final ouster. It is asserted that Fouche´ who had been left in charge in Paris during the Battle of Waterloo, was not at all surprised by the news of Napoleon's defeat at Waterloo. The Wikipedia alleges that Fouche´ acted as a double agent during Napoleon's 'hundred days.' Fouche´ was also one of those who insisted on Napoleon's second and final abdication. Could Fouche´ and the other French deputies have been bribed or coerced by Louis XVIII's agents in a Royalist plot, with the money being advanced by the Rothschilds? This is quite plausible, as after Napoleons' escape from Elba, before Waterloo, besides the British and the Prussians, the Austrians and the Russians had also decided to mobilize against Napoleon at the Congress of Vienna. It would thus have been quite difficult for Napoleon, with his now diminished resources to have defeated the entire European Coalition, even if he had succeeded at Waterloo. Some of the French political and military leaders could have feared retribution from the Royalists in case of Napoleon's final defeat, and hence could have connived at the Fall of Napoleon. It is even alleged that the European Bankers preferred to lend money for the Allied Cause against Napoleon, after the Retreat from Moscow (1812).

It is alleged that Nathan Mayer Rothschild (one of the sons of the Founder, Amschel Mayer Rothschild) the great Jewish banker in London, made a very great fortune at the London Stock Exchange just after Waterloo, as he most unscrupulously spread the initial fake news that Napoleon had won the battle, which led to a great drop in the value of the shares to his advantage. It is alleged that Nathan had received the news – by carrier pigeon or by other means--of Napoleon's defeat at Waterloo, even before the British government (there could be some truth in this assertion, as the entire Rothschild family of bankers made their fortune by the wars of the French Revolution, followed by the Napoleonic War, from 1792-1815 (The New Encyclopaedia Britannica, 1997). The same source has also stated that Nathan Rothschild in London and James (Jakob) Rothschild in Paris were the smartest of the four Rothschild brothers, and so the above-mentioned allegation of unscrupulous trading does not appear to be far-fetched.

So, as a result of Waterloo, Britain became an unchallenged superpower and world hegemon, financially and economically, because of which it was boastfully asserted that "The sun never sets on the British Empire!" However, it should be realized that the British Empire, unlike the Roman Empire, lacked cohesion and permanence, as it lasted only for 150 years, quite unlike the Western Roman Empire's 500 years duration, and the Eastern Roman Empire's additional 500-800 years, as a great power, until the Fall of Constantinople. Constantinople easily fell to the Turks in 1453 CE, due to its weakening as a result of the Crusades, and also due to the refusal of Western Europe to send timely aid to Constantinople due to the Great Schism between the Western and Eastern Churches since the 11th century CE.

Coming back to the subject of the British Empire, it is indeed ironical and ludicrous that the 'great' British war-time Premier, Winston Churchill, made a grandiose speech during the Battle of Britain in 1940, while complimenting the Royal Air Force by saying, "if the British Empire were to last a **thousand years**, men would still say, 'This was their finest hour!' " **In actual fact, the British Empire lasted less than ten years, as India, 'the Jewel in the Crown' (which was won by Britain by fraud and treachery at the Battle of Plassey in 1757) had to be granted its independence in 1947 by Clement Attlee's Labour Government, mainly due to Britain's financial bankruptcy**.

Regarding the role of the Rothschilds in providing a pivot for the future formation of the State of Israel, we shall later meet with Lord Lionel Walter Rothschild, the son of Nathan Rothschild, in the Balfour Declaration of 1917, as **the original letter of the Declaration was addressed to Lord Rothschild, who was the head of the Jewish**

community in Britain. Thus, the Rothschild family has ever since been taking the credit for the creation of the State of Israel (contrary to the arguments of Christian Zionists, who claim that it was God who intervened in the creation of the present Zionist State of Israel).

The Balfour Declaration, which came a hundred years after Waterloo, was only an outworking of Britain's arrogance, as Britain felt that she could barter away any land conquered by her to anyone she pleased (in this case, Palestine to be given over to the Jews of Europe) in case it served Britain's strategic and financial interests very well.

The Second Driving Force to The Present Conflict: The Rise of Revolutionary Movements in Europe and the World :

Shortly after the Napoleonic War, revolutionary movements for independence sprang up all over Europe and South America (Simon Bolivar). In 1821 the Greeks fought for their independence from the Ottoman Empire, and were greatly aided by the major colonial powers of Britain and France. Even Lord Byron, the famous English poet, who wrote the immortal poem starting with the line, "The isles of Greece, The isles of Greece!" joined in the conflict on the Greek side.

When thinking of Palestine from the European perspective the Crusades readily come to mind, even though they were largely unsuccessful. Even though the initiator of the Crusades, Pope Urban II at Clermont in France, thought mainly on religious lines for the control of Palestine, the Christian kings and nobility would have also thought of political and geo-strategic advantages, such as better trade conditions with the East, for which Venice had the monopoly. Early in the 19th century, in the hey-day of British supremacy, it was easier to think of another 'crusade,' easier of accomplishment, and to put the European proxy, the Jew, into Palestine, in the interest of British imperialism.

An earlier minor plan for a Jewish Crusade to Palestine:

It is of interest to the present discussion that three centuries before Waterloo, two Portuguese Jews in the early 16th century, by the names of David Reubeni and Solomon Molcho tried to stir up the Messianic expectation of the Jews. They wanted to lead a Jewish expedition to Palestine, under royal patronage, but lost their lives after being tried for heresy (Wikipedia).

The Third Driving Force to the Present Conflict: The Advent of the Christian Zionist Movement in 1831 :

Here, we have to consider the early Christian Zionists, such as the British Bible teacher and commentator, John Nelson Darby (1800-1882) and the later American dispensationalist, Cyrus I. Scofield (1843-1921).

John Nelson Darby was an Anglo-Irish clergyman in the Anglican Church of Ireland. He belonged to an elite family which was well-connected with the British Establishment.

As a result of his family's connexion with Horatio Nelson (the greatest of English admirals—who first saved India for Britain by destroying the French fleet at the Battle of the Nile in 1799, and then saved Britain itself from a Napoleonic invasion in 1805 at the Battle of Trafalgar) Darby was given the second name of Nelson, at his baptism. Darby was the first British Bible teacher to propound his hare-brained doctrine of the unbelieving and unregenerate Jewish race to be the true inheritor of God's promises made to Abraham. He even went on to state that the promises of Restoration to the Promised Land made by the Old Testament prophets were not to be spiritually applied to the Church, but actually applied only to the physical descendants of Abraham. All this in spite of the entire New Testament teaching to the contrary, and the fact that the Jewish race continued to reject Jesus of Nazareth as their long-awaited Messiah. In all this, Darby was essentially refusing to accept the Replacement Theology, held by the universal Church from its beginning, that the Church has replaced Israel, due to Israel's unbelief, and rejection of Christ as the promised Messiah. Darby replaced the Replacement Theology with his new-fangled Restoration Doctrine.

Darby also perfected his Dispensational doctrine of the Jewish race's uncontested right to Palestine, and their future prophetic role. **In order to justify Israel's role in prophecy before Christ's Second Coming, Darby propounded a totally new doctrine of the Secret Rapture of the Church before the Great Tribulation (not to be found anywhere in Scripture). After the Secret Rapture, the prophetic clock would start ticking for Israel, which would go through the Great Tribulation, alone and without the Church, and act as Christ's evangelists (also not taught in Scripture). There would also be a literal Millennium of a thousand years, with Christ ruling over the world from Jerusalem, along with Israel as a Nation (Not found in Revelation ch. 20, the only New Testament reference to the Millennium).**

Prior to this, Darby was very conscientious where the interests of the British public were under consideration, because, even though he had previously studied law, he refused to practise it stating that "as a lawyer, I may be compelled to do injustice to some individual or the other." Darby, accordingly became a clergyman, but later resigned due to a conflict of loyalties. Soon after Darby's resignation it is alleged that he sustained a serious accident due to a fall from a horse (Wikipedia). Darby drastically changed his theological views shortly after the accident, not only about Church government (Ecclesiology) but also about the prophecies of the End Times (Eschatology). Darby was the most prominent member of the Plymouth Brethren movement at its inception in 1831. In case Darby had restricted himself to ecclesiology, and to the spread of the Brethren Movement alone, then no great harm would have been done. It is most unfortunate that Darby did not care to realize the 'mountains of injustice' which would accrue to the native Palestinian Arabs, and the 'rivers of blood' that would flow in Palestine in case his Restoration scheme were realized, and the Jews were forcefully thrust in to Palestine. **As usual, for the 'white supremacist' West, the natives of Asia, Africa, America (North and South), Australia, New Zealand, and the islands of the sea are hardly to be considered at all, and any atrocity being perpetrated on them could be easily written off as a collateral damage (with hardly any questions asked, as in Gaza in 2023-25).** The greatest harm was done by Darby to the unity of the Church and to world peace by his totally erroneous eschatology, which led to the World Zionist Movement in the late 19th century, to the Balfour Declaration of 1917, and finally to the formation of the State of Israel on 15th May 1948, with its unending conflict in the Middle East ever since.

It is indeed interesting to note that prior to the early 19th century, before Britain became a formidable superpower, no Bible teacher anywhere in the British Isles had proposed such a Restoration Theology, during a period when Britain lacked the military means of opposing the Ottoman Empire in Palestine. Hence, when Darby proposed his new Restoration Doctrine, we could infer that he may very well have been consciously or subconsciously influenced by geo-political factors of British supremacy and superiority. This could have led him to seek for Bible texts in justification, especially from the Old Testament, as hardly any are to be found in the New Testament.

Darby was considered very controversial in his lifetime, and was criticized by some or many of his contemporaries, such as Charles Haddon Spurgeon, the Baptist 'prince of preachers.' Spurgeon considered that Darby and the Plymouth Brethren had defective views about Christ's unique sacrifice once for all time, on the cross. Spurgeon also referred to Darby's doctrines as

being 'warped, divisive, and dangerously innovative' ((Wikipedia).

The second most influential Christian Zionist was Cyrus I. Scofield, who popularized the Dispensational Teaching in America with his publication of the Scofield Reference Bible in 1909. This Bible was profusely interlaced with Scofield's dispensational notes, so that the reader might have even considered that the notes themselves were the equivalent of Gospel truth.

The term 'dispensationalism' was coined in 1928 by a critic, Philip Mauro, in his book entitled, "The Gospel of the Kingdom." Mauro stated the following: "Evangelical Christianity must purge itself from the leaven of dispensationalism," by which he referred to the "new premillennialism, the idea of dispensational timing, and the Israel-Church distinction merged in to a singular bundled idea."

The Presbyterian minister, J.W. Bowman referred to the Scofield Bible as "the most dangerous heresy current to be found within Christian circles."

Kevin Philips, the American political analyst has claimed in the journal, "American Theocracy" in 2006 that the fundamentalist Christian Zionist lobby in America, along with the American oil lobby fully supported and encouraged President George W. Bush's invasion of Iraq in 2003. N.B. In case this is true, then they have much to answer for in the tens of thousands of Iraqi lives lost, along with the utter destabilization of Iraq, and the subsequent rise of the terrorist organization, the ISIS. [It has been stated now on You Tube that the prime instigator for America's meddling in Iraq was Netanyahu (or some other Israeli leader), who 'convinced' the American Congress that all the problems of the Middle East would be solved in case Saddam Hussein were removed!] **Philips has further pointed out that most theologians today do not agree with dispensational eschatology. They have also stated that the**

Bible does not give a specific sequence of end-time events, or in other words a clear and unambiguous timeline of prophetic events. Such a belief is the result of a century of amplified 'Darbyism.'

So much so for J.N. Darby and his Christian Zionism, which has spurred such a cold, bellicose theology, which is as different from the warmth of Christ's teachings, especially the Sermon on the Mount, as the cold and lifeless moon is different from the blazing sun.

The Fourth Driving Force to The Present Conflict: The Secular World Zionist Movement of The Late 19th Century:

This movement was started by Theodor Herzl, an Austro-Hungarian secular Jewish journalist and lawyer, who took his inspiration and motivation from the preceding Christian Zionist movement of J.N. Darby and others. At that time, the Jews were being persecuted in many European countries, including Russia (unlike in Muslim and Arab countries, including Palestine, where the Jews were reasonably well tolerated). The persecutions reached their culmination in the Dreyfus Affair in France, which earned considerable notoriety not only in France, but all over Europe.

Alfred Dreyfus, a French-Jewish artillery officer was unfairly charged with selling military secrets to Germany. Dreyfus was made the scapegoat in order to protect other high-ranking officials, including the Hungarian Count Esterhazy. Dreyfus was sentenced to penal solitude in Devil's Island in 1894.

The Dreyfus Affair convinced Herzl and other Zionists that they would never be safe any longer in Europe. So, the persecuted Jews should have their own homeland. Herzl, an avowed atheist, organized the First World Zionist Congress in Basel, Switzerland in 1897. Various proposals and countries were considered. However, the

doctrine of the Christian Zionists, that Palestine belonged to the Jews, won the day, and henceforth the Zionists were not satisfied with anything less than Palestine itself.

The Fifth Driving Force to The Present Conflict: The Start of The First World War in August 1914:

In this War the Allies: Britain, France and Czarist Russia were pitted against the Central Powers of Germany, Austria and the Ottoman Empire (Turkey).

Early in the War, there was a stalemate on the Western Front and the Western Allies and Germany dug in for a form of Trench warfare, with heavy casualties on both sides. The British, under Winston Churchill, the First Lord of the Admiralty, decided to attack the soft under-belly of the Ottoman Empire at the Gallipoli Peninsula (adjacent to the Dardanelles strait). As this daring naval advance was not sufficiently backed up by British ground troops (partly due to the alleged hesitation of Lord Kitchener, the British Secretary of War, to fully commit the army reserves: Wikipedia), the venture proved to be a disaster.

The British had not, however, given up the idea of the soft under-belly to attack the Ottomans. This time they chose to fight in Palestine. However, as the British were not confident of an unaided victory, they decided to seek the help of the Arabs of the Middle East and Palestine, who were under Ottoman rule. The British promised the Arabs their independence after the War, and promised to make the Emir, Hussein Sharif of Mecca, as king of the Arabs (This Agreement is contained in the Correspondence between Sir Henry MacMahon--the British High-Commissioner in Cairo--and the Emir of Mecca, known as the MacMahon-Hussein Sharif Correspondence, of 1915-1916).

On these terms, the Arabs enthusiastically helped the British leader, the young Lawrence of Arabia, to defeat the Ottomans. In 1917, after driving out the Ottomans with

Arab help, General Allenby triumphantly rode into Jerusalem, 'without firing a shot.'

It was indeed very unfortunate for the Arabs to have trusted 'perfidious Albion' (Britain), because as usual, Britain was quite prepared to make and break treaties whenever it suited her interest (This was the way, by treachery and fraud, that Britain first got a foothold into India at Plassey in 1757, and it was also the way she gradually gained the whole subcontinent, by a concerted policy of 'divide and rule'). **In hindsight, we could confidently assert that the Palestinian Arabs would have remained much better off under Ottoman rule, when they peacefully lived in their own homes and country.** Thus, as a result of helping Britain to win the war, the poor Palestinian Arabs (Muslims and Christians) have had the indignity of handing over their lands and possessions to the alien Zionist Jews, who had been driven out of Palestine 2000 years earlier, and were being hounded out from Europe, where they had never been allowed a peaceful resting place (unlike in all parts of the Muslim and Arab world and in India, where the Jews were unmolested).

The Sixth Driving Force to the Present Conflict: The Iniquitous Sykes-Picot Accord :

As already stated, Britain had no intention of carrying out the promises made to the Arabs, and just a year later, in 1916 Britain and France made the **Sykes-Picot Accord,** in which they decided that after the war was over, they would divide up the Middle East between them, with Britain gaining control of Palestine and Iraq, and France ruling over Lebanon and Syria. This Accord and decision was made without informing the Arab leaders, who were still very busy fighting the Ottomans on behalf of Britain.

The Seventh Driving Force to The Present Conflict: The Balfour Declaration of November 1917:

By early 1917, the War against Germany was going badly on the Western front. Russia, after the Communist Revolution, had already withdrawn from the war on the eastern front, and America had not yet entered on the Allied side. At least three reasons are given for the Balfour Declaration, and all could be correct:

1. Chaim Weizmann, a British-Jewish chemist, helped in the production of Tri-Nitro-Toluene (needed for explosives) by an alternative method. When asked to state his reward Weizmann insisted on being granted a Jewish Homeland in Palestine.
2. There were many Jews among the Russian Bolsheviks, and it was surmised by the British that in case the incentive of a Jewish Homeland were offered, then Russia might be willing to re-enter the war, and open up a second, eastern front against the Germans.
3. It was felt that in case of the promise of a Jewish Homeland then the powerful and wealthy Jewish lobby in America would not only financially help the allied war effort, but might also persuade America to enter the war (It is true that America entered the War against Germany in April 1917, but the proposals for the Balfour Declaration would have been initiated long before the actual Declaration in November 1917).

Some in the British War Cabinet were Christian Zionists, such as the Prime Minister, David Lloyd George. However, religious reasons were only secondary to the geo-political situation not often discussed. There was a strategic reason for Britain's Zionist cause in Palestine, viz. control of the Suez Canal, by a British proxy, the European Jew. This control of the Suez Canal was vital for Britain to hold on to India, the 'Jewel in the Crown.'

America did come in to the war in April 1917, but before the Balfour Declaration was made America and France were also consulted, and both gave their consent. None of them considered the future problems for the native Palestinians, or for the possibility of future conflicts in the Middle East. All of them had a closed, colonial and racist mindset.

When the Declaration was made, (and named after the British Foreign Secretary, Arthur James Balfour) the lone dissenting member of the British Cabinet was ironically the only Jew in the cabinet, Lord Montague. His objection was that after a Jewish homeland was created in Palestine, the Jewish diaspora spread all over the world might suffer hardships and discrimination, as some countries might compel Jews to migrate to Israel. **Montague also argued that the Jews were a race and not a nation, and so finding a Homeland for the Jews was quite unnecessary (Avi Shlaim, Video, Bibliography No. 2). N.B. Montague did consider the possible adverse repercussions for the Jewish diaspora, but it is not mentioned whether Montague considered or stated about the very likely adverse repercussions for the Palestinian Arabs!**

The Balfour Declaration was addressed to Lord Lionel Walter Rothschild, the leader of the Jewish community in Britain. The letter clearly stipulated that apart from providing a homeland for the Jews, that a) The native Palestinians (existing non-Jewish communities in Palestine) would be permitted to live in peace, and their rights would be respected. b) Jews outside Palestine would not be compelled to emigrate to Israel.

It is indeed very unfortunate that though point b) has been adhered to and the worldwide Jewish diaspora has not suffered much, the same cannot be said about point a), because by contrast, the local Palestinians have suffered horrendous injustice for more than one hundred years.

The Balfour Declaration (Full text)

Dear Lord Rothschild:

I have much pleasure in conveying to you, on behalf of His Majesty's Government [of King George V], the following declaration of sympathy with Jewish Zionist aspirations, which has been submitted to and approved by the Cabinet. His Majesty's Government views with favour the establishment in Palestine of a national home for the Jewish people, and will use their best endeavours to facilitate the achievement of this object, it being clearly understood that nothing shall be done which may prejudice the civil and religious rights of existing non-Jewish communities in Palestine, or the rights and political status enjoyed by Jews in any other country.

I would be grateful if you would bring this declaration to the knowledge of the Zionist Federation.

Yours sincerely,

Arthur James Balfour.

In fact, it can be stated without contradiction, that the Balfour Declaration is one of the greatest travesties, and one of the most unjust of declarations in world history. It is rightly called a Declaration (unilateral) and not an Agreement, as the Palestinians were never consulted. This Declaration has never been accepted by the Arabs, and hence all the subsequent non-cooperation by the Arab nations for any settlement with the Jews of Palestine, and their open hostility and belligerence towards the State of Israel, ever since its inception in 1948.

The Eighth Driving Force to The Present Conflict: The End of World War I, and Britain's being given the Mandate to rule Palestine by the newly-formed League of Nations in July 1922 :

Britain decided to incorporate the Balfour Declaration in to their Mandate for governing Palestine. They encouraged many of the European Jews to migrate to Palestine. Prior to the Balfour Declaration the Jews constituted only 10 per cent of the population of Palestine, and they owned only 2 per cent of the land (Avi Shlaim, video). Netanyahu and his team now want the whole land for themselves, and nothing for the Palestinians. **The story of the camel and the Arab is being replicated all over again, not only figuratively but also literally. This has been initiated and supported by 'perfidious Albion' (Britain), and is now being perfected and brought to fruition by 'Uncle Sam' (America), who is the chief scion and offshoot of Britain, and so could be expected to behave in like manner as the parent.**

With the increasing influx of Jews in to Palestine, the Jewish population went up to 27 per cent within 17 years. The inevitable backlash came in the form of riots by the Arabs in the Middle East, and these riots and revolts were suppressed with great brutality by the British, who sometimes used the Indian army in the process.

Faced with increasing conflict, the British decided to restrict and then stop further Jewish immigration. They issued a 'White Paper' to this effect in May 1939. This was not liked either by world Jewry or by the Jewish settlers (who complained most unfairly that Britain was being partial to the Palestinians). As a result, some of the Jews also became terrorists, just like some of the earlier Palestinian Arabs.

During their Mandate in Palestine, the British were very partial to the Jewish settlers, and gave them a measure of autonomy in self-government. Moreover, the British utilized the Jewish militias, trained by them, in the further prosecution of the war against Germany in the Middle East, during the Second World War. By contrast, all these advantages were denied to the Palestinian Arabs. Thus, when Israel declared itself as a nation in 1948, they had all the advantages, and were well prepared economically and militarily to survive (with Western help), unlike the Arabs, who continued to be dependent on outside help. Part of this favouritism by the British could be explained by the non-cooperation by the Palestinian Arabs, leading to their further alienation and deprivation.

The Ninth Driving Force to The Present Conflict: Creation of the State of Israel in 1948, preceded and followed by the *Nakba* (or forcible eviction of the Palestinians):

By 1946, Britain found it increasingly hard to govern Palestine due to the prolonged Arab-Israeli conflict, culminating in the explosion at the King David Hotel, by Jewish terrorists led by Menachem Begin. The next year (1947), the British handed over the Mandate for Palestine to the newly-formed United Nations, which decided as per an earlier British recommendation to partition Palestine in to an Israeli state and a Palestinian state. This plan of partition was vehemently opposed by all the Arab countries, and all the Palestinian Arabs.

The next year on 15th May 1948 (on the very day after Britain's Mandate had expired), the Jewish settlers decided to take matters in to their own hands. It is alleged that Israel first of all forcefully evicted, expelled and dispossessed 750, 000 Palestinian Arabs, in the most brutal and barbaric manner, and forced them to become refugees (figure provided by Avi Shlaim in his video). [It is not very clear whether the *Nakba* preceded or just followed the attack on Israel by the united Arab armies. However, there are indications now in certain books that the Jews had already started expelling Palestinians even before the creation of Israel in May 1948, and shortly after the announcement of the Partition Plan by the UN in 1947 : M. Scott-Baumann, pp. 68-72, "The Shortest History of Israel and Palestine." (Bibliography No.29).] **They then declared themselves as the new Nation State of Israel, with David Ben-Gurion, a Polish Jew, becoming the first Prime Minister.**

The Tenth Driving Force to The Present Conflict: The First Arab-Israeli War of 1948:

The surrounding Arab nations all joined together to destroy Israel as a nation, just after its formation on 15th May 1948. This has already been alluded to, and how Israel came out as the victor, due to extensive help from the Western powers, technological superiority, and lack of coordination among the Arab armies. Moreover, Jordan, which had a well-trained army called the Arab Legion, was well able to take on the Israeli army. The Arab legion prevented the Israeli army from seizing the old City of Jerusalem (East Jerusalem), and also established itself in the West Bank. However, the Arab Legion refused to fight with Israel in the territory demarcated by Israel as its own, nor did this legion aid other Arab armies, such as the Egyptian army. Thus there was disunity in the Arab camp, which was also one of the reasons for Israel's victory during the First Arab-Israeli War of 1948-1949 (M. Scott-Baumann, pp.72-75, Bibliography No. 29).

Christians have been given the false narrative of the 'aggression' of the Arab nations, without being informed about the preceding *Nakba,* and also about all the injustice meted out to the Palestinians by the Balfour Declaration and after (not excluding the unfulfilled promise of Arab independence given by the British in 1915).

The Second Arab- Israeli War in 1956, also called the Suez crisis:

This occurred just after Nasser, the Egyptian President, decided to nationalize the Suez Canal. This action was inimical to the interest of the declining colonial powers Britain and France. Both these countries attacked Egypt, and were joined by their new friend and proxy, Israel, which did just what was wanted by the former colonial powers (**please do remember that the main hidden agenda of the British Prime Minister in favouring the Balfour Declaration, was that the new State of Israel should protect the Suez Canal against any hostile force in the region).**

The advance of the three allies, Britain, France and Israel ended in a fiasco, as an escalation was feared with the Soviet Union. The attack was called off, on the express orders of the US President, Dwight D. Eisenhower, who also wanted to prevent the Arab nations from allying with the Soviet Block.

The Third Arab-Israeli War of June 1967 (The Six-Day War) :

Israel started this war without provocation, destroyed the Air Force of the surrounding Arab nations, in pre-emptive strikes on them before even war was declared. Israel won this war within six days, and took over the West Bank, Gaza, the Golan heights and East Jerusalem, and even after the lapse of 58 years [till now in 2025] has held on to most of these territories.

There have been other wars such as the Yom Kippur war in 1973, in which the Arab nations attacked Israel when Israel was unprepared, in a replica of what Israel had done in 1967. After an initial setback, Israel recovered its losses, largely with American help in equipment and shared intelligence, after a massive American air lift in favour of Israel. But when the Israeli army tried to cross the Suez Canal into Egypt, President Richard Nixon stopped them (reminiscent of what President Dwight D. Eisenhower had done in 1956, during the Suez crisis). **And so, the Middle East conflict goes on, with no end in sight.**

Chapter 9
Conclusion

According to Avi Shlaim, a celebrated Israeli historian at Oxford University, the Israeli-Palestinian conflict is not a conflict of race or religion. It is a conflict of Arab nationalism versus Israeli nationalism. Avi Shlaim (Video in 2024) has also stated that of 2.3 million Palestinian residents of Gaza 1.9 million residents have been displaced. **HE WONDERS WHETHER ISRAEL IS PERPETRATING ANOTHER** *NAKBA* **IN GAZA REMINISCENT OF THE** *NAKBA* **OF 1948?**

We should well ask ourselves, who are acquainted with the Jesus of the Gospels, as to whose side He would be on, if He were to come now as the Judge and Arbiter, whether of the militant and jingoistic Israel and the West, or of the 'underdog,' the poor, dispossessed Palestinian refugee? The answer is so obvious that I do not need to state it!

I would also like to make another categorical assertion:

We are once again being given the choice that Pontius Pilate gave the Jews, whether to prefer Jesus of Nazareth or Barabbas (the militant murderer and anarchist)?

In my considered, Christian opinion, the 'hard-core' Christian Zionists, that is those who would like to support Israel at all costs and regardless of facts, are more neo-colonial than Christian. They have, in a sense, actually decided to favour Barabbas over Jesus of Nazareth!

I have written all this in order to persuade my fellow Christians, and people of other faiths, regarding the truths of the Bible and most of the historical facts related to this important subject of the Arab-Israeli Conflict so that they could form their own unbiased judgment. In

case even a few, or many Christian Zionists, and others could be persuaded to see the Zionist State of Israel for what it really is, and to love the displaced and dispossessed Palestinian Arabs, as Jesus loves them, and not view them as the adversary, then this book of mine would have been abundantly justified.

Another very important reason for my writing this book is that in my view it is now high time for action and not for words, regarding a Two-State solution (or a One-State solution). Israel should be compelled to live (within its pre-1967 borders), peacefully side by side with the Palestinians.

All further attempts by the USA and Britain to continue vetoing or abstaining in favour of Israel should either be neutralized or countered with a firm hand. ***The nations of the Global South should join with Russia and China (two superpowers, each of them equal to America militarily)—a sort of 'Global Action Committee' (without the former colonial nations)--and compel a just resolution of this conflict.***

The formation of the State of Israel in 1948, though of illegal origins (as I perceive it) is a *fait accompli,* and in my view, Israel should only be compelled to live within its pre-1967 borders, and to relinquish East Jerusalem, which they forcefully took from Jordan and the Palestinians in 1967. Moreover, Israel should no longer have the right to harass or subjugate the Palestinians. I am not at all arguing for the abolition of the State of Israel (which the surrounding Arab and Muslim nations desired in the past, due to emotional reasons, and also to meet the strict ends of justice, keeping in view all the preceding geo-political events which were always loaded in favour of Israel and continued Jewish immigration).

IT COULD WELL BE ARGUED BY SOME THAT AS THE STATE OF ISRAEL WAS ESTABLISHED BY THE MOST ILLEGAL, COLONIAL AND PERFIDIOUS

BALFOUR DECLARATION, THIS SAME STATE OF ISRAEL COULD ALSO BE DEMOLISHED BY SIMILAR MEANS.

HOWEVER, THIS IS NOT MY VIEW, NOT OUT OF ANY SYMPATHY FOR ISRAEL, BUT BECAUSE NOW AFTER 77 YEARS OF THE FORMATION OF THE STATE OF ISRAEL, IT IS AN IMPRACTICABLE PROPOSITION.

IT IS TO BE CLEARLY UNDERSTOOD THAT I AM MAKING A CLEAR DISTINCTION BETWEEN JUDAISM AND ZIONISM (OR THE POLITICAL ISRAEL). I AM FULLY MINDFUL OF THE INCALCULABLE DEBT WE GENTILE CHRISTIANS OWE TO THE PATRIARCHS AND PROPHETS OF THE OLD TESTAMENT AND TO THE APOSTLES OF THE NEW TESTAMENT (ALL OF THEM BEING REDEEMED HUMAN BEINGS), BESIDES OUR LORD AND SAVIOUR JESUS CHRIST (WHO WAS BOTH HUMAN AND DIVINE)—ALL OF THEM BEING ORTHODOX JEWS.

I would like to add, that as there are numerous organizations, existing among Jews and Christians for aiding Israel, even so, one or more new organizations should be formed for helping the Palestinians in all possible practical ways, with materials, finances, and voluntary service, if feasible. 'Friends of Palestine' societies should spring up all over, including 'Prayers for Palestine,' on the same lines as the erstwhile, ' Friends of Israel' and 'Prayers for Israel.'

One of the first steps should be to recognize the State of Palestine. [It is indeed heartening to learn that an overwhelming majority of countries in the UN (140 countries) has done so. However, the 'fly in the ointment' is America, which continues to impose its veto on behalf of the Israeli lobby—the American Israeli Public Affairs Committee (AIPAC)—which continues to fund the elections of American politicians, and in the words of the

Republican Congressman Thomas Massie, "AIPAC has provided a 'baby sitter' for every Republican Congressman, in order to oversee their actions and speeches."

Most unfortunately, Palestine only enjoys an Observer Status at present, in the UN General Assembly. All attempts by the majority of the nations in the General Assembly to integrate Palestine as a full member are always vetoed by America in the Security Council on behalf of AIPAC and of Israel. Thus, America has long ago lost the moral high ground in the world's opinion, and its foreign policy seems to cry out, 'Israel first, and America only second!']. How are the mighty fallen! (2 Sam. 1: 19 b, RSV).

Another important step should be that even though Israel and America owe full reparations to Gaza, all people and nations of goodwill could also help in the re-construction of Gaza, out of a feeling of joint solidarity. [It is heartening to learn that several countries—mainly Muslim—have volunteered to re-build Gaza.]

All the peoples of the earth, of whatever country, race or religion, who are large-hearted, and deeply concerned about our common humanity and shared values should look forward to the day, and also help in its emergence, when all the countries of the world:

"... will beat their swords into plowshares and their spears into pruning hooks.

Nation will not take up sword against nation, nor will they train for war anymore.

Come, O house of Jacob, let us walk in the light of the LORD" (Isaiah 2: 4c-5).

"Amen. Come, Lord Jesus." (Revelation 22: 20 b).

Glossary 1

(Geo-political and Historical Events relating to the Israel-Palestine Conflict)

1. The MacMahon-Sharif Correspondence (1915-1916):

In 1915, during the height of World War I, Britain decided to enlist the help of the Arabs to fight against the Ottomans in Palestine. With this goal in view, Sir Henry MacMahon, the British High Commissioner in Cairo, met Husayn Ibn Ali Sharif, the Emir of Mecca and promised to grant independence to the Arabs immediately after the War, and to make the Emir King of the Arabs, provided the Arabs would side with the British against the Ottomans in Palestine. The Emir, as well as the Arab community readily agreed to help the British on these terms.

With Arab help, the young British commander, 'Lawrence of Arabia' was able to drive out the Ottomans from Palestine, due to which General Allenby was able to ride triumphantly in to Jerusalem in 1917 (before the end of the World War) 'without firing a shot.'

Very unfortunately for the Arabs, the Palestinians, and also for the future peace of the Middle East, the British reneged on their promise, and those Palestinian Arabs who aided the British, only helped to 'dig their own graves,' as after 1922 (the year of Britain's Mandate for Palestine), they had to increasingly make way for the immigrant Jews of Europe, and after 1948 to be dispossessed, and driven out as refugees.

2) The Sykes-Picot Accord of 1916 :

'Perfidious Albion' (Britain), had no intention of honouring its promise made to the Arabs a year earlier (the same

Arabs who risked their lives for Britain's hegemony in Palestine), and in 1916 signed the Sykes-Picot Accord with France to carve out the Middle East between these two colonial nations. **The irony was that this new accord was made while the Palestinian Arabs were fighting 'tooth and nail' for the British against the Ottomans, and had no inkling of Britain's duplicity and treachery**. [In fact, India was gained by the same treacherous means by the British in 1757, when the young and inexperienced Nawab of Bengal, Siraj-ud-Daulah, was attacked and overthrown at the Battle of Plassey, even though a treaty of non-aggression and mutual help existed between the Nawab and the East India Company. Moreover, the commander of the Nawab's cavalry, the traitor, Mir Jaffar, and the Jagat Seth bankers of Bengal were drawn into a conspiracy with Robert Clive to replace the Nawab with Mir Jaffar, after the Nawab's proposed overthrow (William Dalrymple, "The Anarchy,"pp. 118-122, Bibliography No. 28). Mir Jaffar remained inactive during the entire battle (just like Lord Stanley at Bosworth Field in England in the late 15th century, which also led to a change in dynasties: Plantagenet to Tudor). **Here at Plassey, Britain was able to 'filch' a victory in spite of overwhelming odds, and thus, was able to start on her belligerent and avaricious goal of empire building 'through the back door.' This was also similar to the treacherous exploits of the Spanish conquistadores, Cortez and Pizarro, in Mexico and Peru respectively in the early 16th century.** Both of them, and many others like them achieved their ends by fraud and treachery (They were all avid but unknowing followers of the Italian 16th century statesman, Machiavelli, who argued against morality and ethics in politics, and stated categorically that means do not matter, and that the end result if achieved would fully justify the means). **Note that this line of reasoning is totally contrary to morals, ethics and religion, but was followed by almost all the Western European countries during their colonizing spree from the 16th century right up to the 20th century: Portugal,**

Spain, Holland, France, Britain, Belgium, Germany, and Italy. They acted on the premise that no faith should be kept with the natives of foreign lands. This has been the usual feature of European aggrandizement and colonization, from which evil effects many countries in the Global South have still not extricated themselves even till today in the 21st century.]

[VERY UNFORTUNATELY, SUCH OVERT COLONIALISM IS NOT DEAD EVEN IN THE 21st CENTURY, BUT IS REPLACED BY THE NEO-COLONIALISM OF AMERICA AND OTHER EUROPEAN COUNTRIES. THE EFFECT IS THE SAME AS FAR AS IMPOVERISHMENT OF THE GLOBAL SOUTH IS CONCERNED. ISRAEL IS DOING EXACTLY THE SAME ALL OVER THE MIDDLE EAST TODAY, AS A PROXY OF THE WEST.]

3) The Balfour Declaration of November 1917 :

In a bid to get help in various ways for the War Effort from the Jewish communities in Britain. and America, and among the Jewish Russian Bolsheviks, Britain decided to grant a National Home in Palestine for the European Jews, but without consulting the Palestinians, to whom promises had already been made (More details on the Balfour Declaration are to be found in chapter 8, and under the Seventh Driving Force, pp. 105-107).

4) The League of Nations Mandate in 1922 for Britain to rule Palestine:

The newly-formed League of Nations, which was mainly controlled by the colonial nations, gave Britain the Mandate to rule Palestine. The British incorporated the Balfour Declaration into their Mandate, and opened up Palestine for immigration to European Jews, who were facing persecution all over Europe and in Russia.

5) The British White Paper of 1939 to limit Jewish immigration:

This was issued by the British in order to prevent further Jewish-Palestinian conflicts, and in order to grant independence to Palestine after ten years. This was opposed by the Jews in Palestine, and also by the Jewish diaspora.

6) The Jewish 'terrorist' group the 'Irgun.'

This group reacted against the 'White Paper' and carried out many acts of terrorism, most notably, blowing up the King David hotel in Jerusalem in 1946, and causing 91 casualties (soldiers and civilians), with many more injured, and with much destruction of the targeted civil records. One of the leaders of 'Irgun' was Menachem Begin (who had come to Palestine earlier, after being released from a Russian prison). The same 'terrorist Begin' was duly rewarded by the Israelis about three decades later when he became the Prime Minister of Israel, and a little later, negotiated peace with Egypt under the Camp David Accord (1979).

7) The Biltmore Hotel, New York, Conference of 1942:

After Britain issued its 'White Paper' the European Jews decided to shift their allegiance to the American Establishment. This was decided at the Biltmore Hotel Conference, at New York in America, with the goal of creating a Jewish Commonwealth in Palestine. This was largely supported by the American political leaders in nexus with Jewish financiers, and one would not be wrong in saying that, "ever since 1942 Uncle Sam has been the fairy god-father of Israel." Money has certainly played its part in these events, due to the influence of the rich Jewish financiers in America---much to the extreme disadvantage of the resident Palestinians.

8) Britain hands over the Mandate for Palestine to the United Nations in 1947:

Faced with increasing difficulty in governing Palestine, as contrary promises were made first to the Palestinians and then to the Jews, and also due to acts of Jewish terrorism, such as the explosion at the King David Hotel in 1946, Britain decided to 'give up' and hand over the Palestinian Mandate to the newly-formed United Nations in 1947.

9) The Decision of the United Nations to Partition Palestine in 1947:

The United Nations, created by, and largely under the control of America and the colonial nations, besides the Soviet Union, decided to partition Palestine between Israel and Palestine, and to award 56 per cent of the land to Israel, even though the Jewish population was less than half that of the Palestinians, even after 25 years of steady Jewish immigration (even in this award, the rampant favouritism and colonial mind set of the Western powers could be made out).

This Partition Plan by the United Nations was never accepted by either the Palestinians or other Arab nations.

10) The Formation of the State of Israel on 15th May, 1948:

Israel unilaterally declared itself as a new nation on 15th May, 1948, the very day after Britain's Mandate ended.

11) The First Arab-Israeli War of May, 1948-1949:

As the increasing presence of the Jews, and the Declaration by Israel of a new nation-state (as well as the preceding *Nakba*) were quite unacceptable to the surrounding Arab nations of Egypt, Jordan and Syria, they all attacked Israel, just after its formation. Most unfortunately for the Palestinian cause the Arabs were soundly defeated by Israel, not only due to immense military support and sharing of intelligence by America, but also due to the disunity, incompetence, and inco-ordination of the Arab armies. Israel's territory was now bigger than what the United Nation had awarded Israel.

(The further Arab-Israeli Wars have been mentioned in chapter 8 and under the title of "The Tenth Driving Force").

12) The *Nakba* or 'Catastrophe':

Before and after the formation of Israel, and also after the attack on Israel by the united Arab armies, the Israeli army systematically expelled 750,000 Palestinians from Israel proper, and sent them out as refugees to Jordan, Lebanon and Syria under the pretext that they could return later (the 'later' of the Israelis has unfortunately never come, and has continued even till today in 2025, as Israel has refused to permit any of the expelled Palestinians to return). Many of the Palestinian families had kept the keys to their houses, for an anticipated return soon. This was a futile exercise, as besides refusing re-entry, the deceitful Israelis demolished the villages, and even uprooted all the trees and other landmarks, so that the once-familiar landmarks were no longer visible.

Those Palestinians who could not be evicted from Israel in to the surrounding Arab nations in 1948 were herded into the narrow Gaza strip, which was part of the Palestinian territory. Ever since then, their children, grandchildren and great-grandchildren have been facing appalling difficulties due to the Gaza blockade by Israel since 2006, and now they have been experiencing a genocide in Gaza for 20 months. **How are the mighty fallen! (2 Sam. 1: 19b, RSV).** From sitting under their own vines and their own fig trees, the poor Palestinians in Gaza are facing abject starvation, due to Israel's unwillingness to let in sufficient food or aid, after already bombing much of the housing, schools and hospitals.

The latest in this tragedy is that both Donald Trump, the American President, and Prime Minister Netanyahu are vying with each other to take over the Gaza strip, after again herding out the Palestinians (where?). Trump has even gone on record to state that he would like to develop Gaza into an Eastern Mediterranean Riviera for tourism (This shows the degradation of American politics, which has now entered its 'nadir,' as the most responsible person of the world's most powerful and rich country thinks first of tourism for his country's personal gain, when the Palestinians in Gaza are struggling for survival and for the most basic necessities that are wantonly denied by Israel).

13) The Camp David Accord of 1978 and The Egypt-Israel Peace Accord of 1979:

This was signed in September 1978 between President Anwar Sadat of Egypt and Prime Minister, Menachem Begin of Israel in the presence of President Jimmy Carter of USA. This led directly to the Egypt-Israel Peace Accord next year in 1979. Thus, President Sadat was the first Arab leader to make peace with Israel. However, this was done at the cost of the Palestinians, and Sadat immediately became a pariah among other Arab nations. Most unfortunately, Sadat was assassinated two years after his Peace Accord with Israel.

14) The First *Intifada* or 'Uprising' (1987-1991, Wikipedia):

This was a non-violent protest by the Palestinians of the West Bank, Gaza strip and Israel Proper in order to pressurize Israel to restore the seized territories of the West Bank by Israel. There were marches and a Civil Disobedience movement. There was occasional violence due to militant groups.

The Palestinian pastor, Munther Isaac, has mentioned about the Two *Intifadas* or Uprisings on pp. 9-11 of his book, " The Other Side of the Wall " (see Bibliography

No.25). Isaac has written about the First *Intifada,* which was largely peaceful: "Life used to stop at 12: 30 pm. There were demonstrations, strikes and street marches with military-imposed curfews. Almost every Palestinian could point to a traumatic moment ... dehumanized by the armed Israeli soldiers and settlers..."

15) The Palestine Liberation Organization (PLO):

The PLO was formed in 1964 to represent the interests of the Palestinian Arabs. Yasser Arafat became its chairman in 1969 (Lexicon Universal Encyclopedia, 1989). The Al Fatah guerilla organization was the most powerful of the diverse groups under the PLO umbrella. The PLO guerillas were compelled to leave Jordan in 1971, and established themselves in Lebanon, from where they were again expelled by Israel in 1982. The PLO was then scattered among other Arab nations.

16) Declaration of the Palestinian State by the Palestinian National Council in November 1988, and their conditional recognition of Israel:

The Palestinian National Council declared a Palestinian State in November 1988, and also conditionally accepted UN Resolution 242, which meant that they were willing to recognize the State of Israel. This was in response to the aspirations of the Palestinians in the First *Intifada,* and also to the fact that Jordan severed all links with the West Bank in July 1988 (Lexicon Universal Encyclopedia).

17) The Second *Intifada* (Wikipedia):

This started from Jerusalem, at the Al-Aqsa Mosque, and lasted sporadically from 2000-2005. Unlike the First *Intifada,* there was continuing violence between the Palestinians and Israeli security personnel. The violence started with the Israeli security forces killing one hundred Palestinian protesters within a few weeks of the commencement of this *Intifada.*

18) The Oslo Accord of September 1993:

This Accord was signed between Yitzhak Rabin, Prime Minister of Israel, and Yasser Arafat, the head of the PLO, in the presence of President Bill Clinton of USA. During the accord, Israel recognized the PLO and the PLO recognized Israel's right to exist, and also renounced militancy. The purpose of the accord was to permit increasing self-government for the Palestinians of the West Bank, with the view of a later Two-State solution. However, on both sides there were people who disagreed.

Very unfortunately, Rabin was assassinated two years later by a right-wing Israeli, who opposed the Oslo Accord. This assassination was followed by Israel's taking a harder line towards the Palestinians, followed by increasing settler colonialism of the West Bank by the Israelis.

19) The Abraham Accords of 2020 (Wikipedia): These accords were signed between Israel and some of the Arab nations in 2020. President Donald Trump initiated these accords between Israel and the UAE, Bahrain and Morocco, in which these Arab nations decided to recognize Israel for the first time, and opened full diplomatic relations with Israel. Most unfortunately for the Palestinians, their long-pending problems did not enter into the equation.

By contrast, Saudi Arabia, possibly due to public opinion, has refused to recognize Israel until the Palestinian problem is solved in a Two-State solution.

20) The Rothschild Family of Bankers:

This was a very influential family of Jewish financiers who made their fortune during the French Revolutionary Wars of the late 18th century, followed by the Napoleonic War of the early 19th century—1792-1815 (New Encyclopaedia Britannica, 1997 and the Lexicon Encyclopedia, 1989). The founding member was Mayer Amschel Rothschild (1744-

1812) who grew up in humbler circumstances in a ghetto in Frankfurt. The family name was derived from the 'red shield' emblem on the door of the family's ancestral home in the ghetto at Frankfurt—'rot' meaning red. By the mid nineteenth century the Rothschilds were the largest European family of bankers. The Rothschilds loaned money to Benjamin Disraeli, the Prime Minister of Britain in 1875 for the purchase of the Suez Canal.

The Balfour Declaration was addressed to one of their descendants, Lord Lionel Walter Rothschild, who was the head of the Jewish community in Britain, in November 1917. The Rothschilds helped to finance some of the early Jewish agricultural communities in Palestine.

(Some other details about the Rothschild Family can be found in chapter 8, and under the heading ,"The First Driving Force," pp. 94-97).

21) Hamas (Wikipedia):

A Sunni Muslim political resistance movement, which has governed Gaza since 2007. Their militia consists of the Qassam Brigade.

22) Hezbollah:

A Shia militant group in southern Lebanon, which forms a 'state within a state.' This group is closely allied with Iran. It was established when Israel invaded Lebanon in the 1980s.

23) The Houthis:

Also called Ansar Allah, it is a Shia militia in Yemen, which refused to abandon the besieged Palestinians in Gaza (unlike the very-rich Gulf States) and put up a tough fight against Israel, during the height of the Gaza genocide, by directing missiles against Israel, and closing the Red Sea to Israeli shipping. Moreover, the Israeli port of Eilat on the Red Sea had to close down for almost one year. Even 'Uncle

Sam' (the self-appointed 'policeman of the world') was obliged to retreat due to the Houthi missiles on American ships, and President Trump was the first to declare a ceasefire, after first of all waging an all-out war against Yemen and the Houthis.

Glossary 2

(Biblical Doctrines relating to the Last Things at Christ's Second Coming : Eschatology)

1) The First Coming of Christ:

The purpose of Christ's First Coming: "Here is a trustworthy saying that deserves full acceptance: Christ Jesus came into the world to save sinners--" (1 Timothy 1: 15).

Jesus Christ was born in 4 BCE in Bethlehem of Judaea (Israel) of the Virgin Mary (by the miraculous 'virgin birth') as His true Father was God Himself.

Christ was placed in a manger "because there was no room for them in the inn" (Luke 2: 7c).Christ was the most wonderful and most holy of anybody who has ever lived. He started His Ministry of three short years at the age of 30 years. He healed the sick, cleansed the leprosy patients, gave sight to the blind, and even raised the dead. His teaching was the most loving teaching about the God of love. Christ enunciated the 'Golden Rule' : " Do to others as you would have them to do to you" (Luke 6: 31), and He preached the highest ethical teaching in the 'Sermon on the Mount' (Matthew chs. 5-7).

The New Testament affirms that Christ lived a perfectly sinless life, and that is why, as God, He could bear all our sins, when He suffered on the Cross for the sins of the whole world – (past, present and future).

Because Jesus challenged the religious Establishment of the worldly and compromising Sadducees, and the harsh, austere and unmerciful Pharisees--the religious leaders of the day--they brought Christ before Pontius Pilate, the Roman Governor of Judaea, and got Christ crucified on

trumped up charges (even though Pilate openly declared that Christ was innocent).

Christ rose again the third day and appeared to His disciples in His resurrected body for 40 days. After the 40 days, Christ ascended into Heaven, after having promised that He would come to earth a Second Time, after an unknown, indefinite period, as King of kings and Lord of lords.

It is indeed ironical that India's revered Father of the Nation, Mahatma Gandhi, had once exclaimed to a Western missionary, words somewhat like these : " You follow one of the most pacific of religious books—the New Testament- and yet the 'Christian' European countries are the most belligerent of nations!" In fact, early in the Church's history, after Church and State were unified under the Roman Emperor, Constantine the topic of 'War' was hotly debated. Only a 'Just War' in self-defence was permitted by the Church. It is most unfortunate that in the one thousand and seven hundred years after Constantine, the European nations have been much more eager to settle their frequent disputes by the 'arbitrement of the sword' rather than by diplomacy, or political and religious dialogue, and thereby to openly deny the truths of the New Testament from Matthew to Revelation. In fact, after 1500 CE the Western European nations have continued on their killing spree of colonizing sovereign, but weaker countries without batting an eyelid, and often by means of deceit and treachery.

In case the countries of Christendom had truly followed Christ's teachings, there would have been fewer wars in Europe, or by Europeans elsewhere in the world, except in extreme cases of self-defence.

2) The Second Coming of Christ (also known as The Second Advent):

This doctrine is clearly taught in almost all the books of the New Testament, and also in certain books of the Old

Testament. It is mentioned in greatest detail in Paul's First Letter to the Corinthians, chapter 15, and in Paul's First letter to the Thessalonians, chapter 4, and verses 13-18. It is also mentioned in the Olivet Discourse of Christ in Matthew chapter 24, Mark chapter 13, and Luke chapter 21. The same subject is also discussed in Luke chapter 17, verses 20-37.

Yes, this same Jesus, who was born 2000 years ago, who was crucified for the sins of the whole world (including all the people who have ever lived, and all who will ever live hereafter), who rose from the dead on the third day, and ascended into heaven about 30 CE, will indeed come a Second Time, with all His angels, and with great power and glory (a glory millions of times more splendid than the greatest potentate who has ever lived—a very poor comparison that could be made between the glory of an earthly ruler and the glory of Christ, is that of the light of a 20-watt electric bulb as compared to the light of the sun just at its fringe 150 million km. distant from the earth!). Christ will take over all the reins of power on earth and in heaven, after He has destroyed Satan.

3) The Great Tribulation:

This is referred to in the Olivet Discourse of Christ. The Great Tribulation is a time of seven years (longer or shorter) towards the end of this age, when it is thought that an evil 'One World Ruler' called antichrist, will arise and rule the world, and carry out horrific atrocities on many people, especially on the true Church of Jesus Christ. This would be a time of indescribable suffering, and Christ has Himself stated that if the duration of the Tribulation were not cut short by God Himself, then nobody could be saved in the Tribulation (Mark 13 : 20).

God's people will be finally saved from the Great Tribulation by the personal appearance of Jesus Christ.

4) Antichrist:

Antichrist will be the One World Dictator who will arise just before the End Times (This interpretation of antichrist is according to the Futurist interpretation of the book of Revelation). He will force the whole world to worship him as God. Antichrist is mentioned in Paul's Second letter to the Thessalonians, chapter 2, and verses 8-9 under the title of "the lawless one." The term antichrist is taken from the First letter of John, chapter 2, verse 18, "Dear children, this is the last hour; and as you have heard that the antichrist is coming, even now many antichrists have come..."

In the book of Revelation, the last book of the Bible, antichrist is referred to as 'the beast' in chapter 13. Also, the term 'mark of the beast' has come from Revelation chapter 13, verses 16-18, where the beast or antichrist compels everyone in the world to take his number, 666, as a mark on the right hand or the forehead, with the goal of total subjugation or economic domination. Those who oppose the beast will be killed, and those who refuse the mark will not be allowed to buy or sell. [We are possibly drawing nearer to that period with our present digital transactions, and forthcoming artificial intelligence, as well as our personal identification numbers, referred to as 'the Aadhar Card' in India.]

There has been much speculation during the last 2000 years as to who could be the antichrist.

The early Christians thought that antichrist could be either Nero or Domitian, two of the most evil and violent and persecuting Roman Emperors of the First century CE. Later on, other great and charismatic historical personages have been thought to qualify. In *War and Peace,* Leo Tolstoy has made one of his Russian heroes consider whether Napoleon Bonaparte, the Ruler of Western Europe, could qualify; and much ingenuity was shown by Tolstoy in making his hero figure out whether Napoleon's name could match the number 666.

In Revelation chapter 19, Christ returns to the world and destroys the beast or antichrist, and rules on earth for one thousand years, in chapter 20 (this is again according to the Futurist, Pre-Millennial interpretation of the book of Revelation).

5) The Millennium:

This is mentioned in detail in Revelation chapter 20. During this time, presumably of one thousand years, Satan will be fully bound and unable to deceive the nations (vv. 2-3). This could be an idyllic time, with changes in nature and in geography. The very carnivores will co-exist with herbivores, and will not molest them. This is mentioned in the Old Testament book of Isaiah, and possibly could be fulfilled during the Millennium, but is merely a conjecture, as such details are not mentioned in chapter 20 of Revelation. During this time, Christ will directly rule over the whole world, along with his martyred and resurrected saints (v.4). However, there is no mention about Israel in Revelation chapter 20, except a cryptic reference to Jerusalem in verse 9.

The Christian Zionist (Dispensational) theologians believe that all the promises made to Israel in the Old Testament prophetic books, such as Isaiah, Jeremiah and Ezekiel, and yet unfulfilled, will be fulfilled during the Millennium for the literal and physical race of Abraham, the Jews of the World (Walvoord, pp. 464-467, and Pentecost, pp. 476-477, see the Bibliography Nos. 22 & 23 respectively).

The three major views about the Millennium—the Pre-Millennial, Post-Millennial and the A-Millennial views are as follows:

a) **The Pre-Millennial View:** Christ's Second Coming ushers in the Millennium i.e. Christ returns to earth *before* the Millennium. The Last Judgment and Heaven commence only after the Millennium.

There are many Christians, who are not Christian Zionists who hold a pre-millennial view.

b) **The Post-Millennial View :** According to this view, the world will become better, and become 'christianized' due to the success of the World Missionary Movements. This preaching of the Gospel leads to the Millennium, or 'Golden Age' and Christ will return only *after* this Millennium. However, two World Wars, and the most horrendous Holocaust in the 20th century have caused this view to fall out of favour.

c) **The A-Millennial view :** There have been many illustrious names who have held this view, such as St. Augustine, the Church Father and theologian of the 4th century CE, and the Protestant leaders such as Luther in the 16th century. There are many evangelical Christians who hold this view in our own day. According to this view there will not be any literal Millennium, and the binding of Satan mentioned in Rev. 20: 2-3 was fulfilled by Christ's death on the Cross, at which time Satan "or the strong man" was bound by Christ (Mt: 12:29) According to this view the Final Judgment and Heaven will commence immediately after Christ's Second Coming.

6) The Rapture of the Church:

The term 'rapture' is derived from a Latin word meaning to be caught up or to go up. The Rapture has been referred to in Paul's First Letter to the Thessalonians chapter 4, verses 14-18. According to this passage, at Christ's Second Coming all believers, dead and alive, will rise up to meet Christ and his angels in the air. All the believers who have died up till then will be resurrected first, and in their new bodies they will rise to meet the Lord in the air. After that will be the turn of the living believers, who without facing death, will receive new resurrection bodies, and will then go to meet the Lord in the air. After that, there will be no more parting from Christ for the believer, as per Paul's conclusion to this passage,

"...And so we will be with the Lord forever. Therefore encourage each other with these words" (vv. 17d-18).

7) Timing of the Rapture:

The usual teaching of the Church since the last 2000 years is that the Rapture will occur after the Great Tribulation, when Christ returns. So, the Church will have to go through and endure the Great Tribulation, as mentioned by Christ in His Olivet Discourse in Matthew chapter 24, and in the parallel passages in the Synoptic Gospels, Mark and Luke. So, this standard, orthodox teaching is referred to as the Post-Tribulation Rapture. Holders of this view could be Pre-Millennial, i.e. the Rapture will usher in the Millennial kingdom of Christ on earth. Equally devout Christians (such as St. Augustine (4h century) and Martin Luther (16th century) have held to the A-Millennial view that there will not be a literal Millennium on earth after the Second Advent, and that believers will go directly to their heavenly home with Christ.

8) The 'Secret Rapture' of Dispensational or Christian Zionist theology:

This view has been held for only the last 200 years, ever since John Nelson Darby propounded his dispensational or Christian Zionist theology, after 1831. According to this view the Church will be exempted from the Great Tribulation. Jesus will come the Second Time secretly for His Church (Stage One), when He will take the Church (dead and living believers) to Himself. The physical seed of Abraham, viz. the Jewish people will go through the Great Tribulation, alone, without the Church. The Jewish people will be Christ's evangelists during the Great Tribulation, and they will suffer very greatly, a time referred to or implied as 'Jacob's or Israel's Trouble' in the book of Daniel (12 : 1b).

Flaws to this view: This view is not taught in Scripture. In the Thessalonians passage already quoted above, Christ's coming is attended by the Voice of the Archangel and with the trumpet of God. These are neither silent, nor secret.

Moreover, this Secret Rapture view envisages that the Second Coming has a Stage Two also, when after the Great Tribulation, Christ returns to the earth along with His Church, before the Millennium. The two stages of the Second Coming are also not taught in Scripture, nor the doctrine of the Pre-tribulation Rapture, as per the verdict of two seasoned theologians (Grudem, pp.1133-1136, and Erickson, pp. 1197-1199, see the Bibliography Nos. 26 & 27 respectively).

9) Dispensational Theology or Christian Zionism:

As mentioned above, this theology was propounded by John Nelson Darby, one of the founders of the Plymouth Brethren in 1831. According to Darby, and the Christian Zionists, the Old Testament promises to Israel in the book of Genesis, and the promises of Israel's Restoration in the Major Prophets: Isaiah, Jeremiah, Ezekiel etc. are to be only applied to the literal and physical race of Abraham and Jacob viz. the Jews. None of these promises apply to the Church. They also believe that Palestine should only belong to the Jews, since God promised it to the Patriarchs. It was this Christian Zionist teaching that made Theodor Herzl, the founder of Zionism in the late 19th century to think of Palestine as the proposed homeland for the Jews. It was this theology that gave Britain and America the excuse for thrusting their proxy, the European Jew, into Palestine and into the heart of the Middle East to carry out their neo-colonial agenda there. This doctrine has led to the 'mountains of injustice' and the 'rivers of blood' to keep flowing in the Middle East ever since the European Jews were artificially re-grafted into their ancient homeland.

(More information on John Nelson Darby is given in chapter 8, and under the sub-heading "The Third Driving Force").

Should We support the present State of Israel? (Relationship of Israel and the Church) Bibliography & Quotations

(Same as published in April 2024, but with additions in 2025)

Introduction: I am not enumerating any of the Christian Zionist books either read by me, or just glanced through, as the Old Testament texts quoted by them in justification, or as 'proof texts' are 'common knowledge,' and can be easily located [April 2024.]

I have relied heavily on certain videos and other information from the internet, and from the Wikipedia. Some important subjects (see below) have been cross-checked by me from the *New Encyclopaedia Britannica*, the 15th edition, and which was updated to 1997, and also from the *Lexicon Universal Encyclopedia*, 1989 (Bibliography Nos. 18-20). All of these sources are being duly acknowledged by me in the following list. Most of these videos give (what I consider to be) a balanced and an unbiased presentation:

A) Videos

1. **Gideon Levy:** Is a dissenting Israeli journalist. He stated in a video in 2015 as follows: "Israel is the only country in the world, where the 'occupier' claims that it is the victim, and that too the only victim!"

2. **Avi Shlaim:** Is a celebrated Israeli historian, now in UK, at Oxford University. His wife is the grand-daughter of Lloyd George, the former British Prime Minister. She is embarrassed by the Balfour Declaration. Shlaim has stated that his ancestors

had lived peacefully in Iraq for many generations, and had no intention of leaving, even after the creation of the State of Israel. Shlaim has alleged that in a bid to create instability, and to coerce the Jews to leave Iraq and migrate to Israel, the Mossad (Israel's secret service) planted a bomb in a synagogue, and spread the rumour that Arab terrorists were responsible.

3. **Rabbi David Feldman** spoke in an Islamic Mosque in solidarity with Gaza.

4. ***Zionism is not the same as Judaism.* This is the title of the video in which Rabbi Yisroel David Weiss has spoken.** One of the two, either Weiss or Feldman has stated that it is blasphemy to consider Israel as a nation state, as God's decree of banishment for the Jews was for perpetuity. Weiss has stated that he does not believe that the State of Israel represents world Jewry. Weiss has also stated that he and some other Jews never keep a flag of Israel, nor do they celebrate the annual Foundation Day of Israel on 15th May.

5. **Ilan Pappe´** : *Ten Myths about Israel* (Video).

6. **Video entitled, "Britain in Palestine—1917-1948."**

7. **Scott Ritter** is a former American Weapons Inspector, and a former Naval Seal. He has also visited the former Soviet Union in order to inspect some of the nuclear weapons there at the time of the 'Détente.' In November 2023 Ritter put out a video entitled : "What Palestine did was justified. What Israel did is pure evil." Ritter has previously visited Israel, and his sympathies used to be previously with Israel. Ritter is not very certain about the future of Israel now, as Israel has created so many enemies, not only among the Arabs, but also in the whole world. Ritter has stated

unequivocally, "I would like the Israeli army to lose so that Israel would be forced to permit a Two-State solution."

8. **Douglas Macgregor** Is a retired US army colonel. Like, Ritter, he is also sympathetic to the plight of the Palestinians. He, like Ritter, has stated that Israel has a right to exist. (More about Macgregor in Myth no.7).

9. **John Mearsheimer** is a respected American Professor and geo-political analyst. He is very sympathetic to the Palestinian cause. He has stated the following: "The train for a Two-State solution has long since left the station." (Meaning that it is now impossible). This would be true only if the *status quo ante* were maintained. I differ with the respected Professor in that in my view, sooner or later, Israel will be compelled to accept a Two-State solution (or even a One-State solution), perhaps by an imaginary 'Global Action Committee' *sans* Israel and the US.

10. **Jeffrey Sachs** is also a respected American Professor, geo-political analyst and a consultant on world affairs at the United Nations. He is regularly invited by many countries for his advice, and for talks and deliberations. In one of his videos, he commented on Netanyahu's avowed goal of 'destroying Amalek.' He has lamented the 'over-literalism' of the Christian Zionists in their interpretation of the Old Testament prophecies in the Bible. He is a Jewish-American, and so his denunciation of Israel carries more weight.

11. **Judge Andrew Napolitano** is in charge of the You Tube channel called "Judging Freedom." The judge has interviewed all the above-mentioned American celebrities (and others also, not only about the Hamas-Israel war, but also about the Ukraine-

Russia war). Judge Napolitano, by his precise and pragmatic interviewing has revealed himself to be a large-hearted, just and conscientious Christian gentleman, just like the other four Americans mentioned by me. All of them appear to be free from prejudice, and have a different narrative to offer as compared to the American Establishment. Jeffrey Sachs, who is so enthusiastic about a Two-State solution, with the capital of Palestine in East Jerusalem (as per the pre-existing 1967 borders) is a Jewish-American. So, it is indeed heartening to know that all is not lost! It is because of such American 'stalwarts' that ordinary people, such as me in the Global South have not completely lost faith in America.

12. **The inimitable George Galloway** is a long-time MP from Scotland, and a leader of the 'Worker's Party' in the UK. He previously won a by-election on the subject of the carnage in Gaza, and even had heated exchanges on the Floor of the House with Premier Rishi Sunak on the subject of Gaza. He has been interviewing people not only on the Gaza Conflict but also on the Ukraine War. He always has his hat on while interviewing others, or while speaking himself. He is unconventional, usually mild and soft-spoken, with his Scotch accent. He is extremely considerate to the person being interviewed, and never interrupts, and even leaves sufficient time after the speaker has finished before asking the next question. In addition, he rarely intrudes his own opinions while interviewing others. [This is the very opposite of what I am used to here in India.]

13. **Pastor David, of the Berean Bible Church** put out a video in November 2023, entitled: *National Israel is NOT God's People* based on the Bible Text, Phil. 3:3. In other words, according to this text, the

Church has replaced Israel as God's people. The pastor has also asserted that as the Jews have been following the later Talmudic Law, and not the original Mosaic Law delivered on Mount Sinai (1400 BCE), they cannot be considered as the true Israel, even in the Old Testament sense.

14. **A video was put out in November-December 2023 by a pastor (name withheld) of the Old Union Presbyterian Church, entitled:** ***Devotion: The Problem with Christian Zionism***. He has pointed out some of the flaws of Christian Zionism, both in its theology and also in the prejudiced attitude of its adherents.

15. **The Video Channel**, "The Lost Signal" : "Was the English Language saved by the Black Death in the 14th century ?" (2025).

16. **Richard Wolff** : An American Professor of Economics.. He put out a video in 2025 "Instances of European Settler Colonialism in the Americas, and now in Palestine."

    He highlighted the fact that the 'Red' Indians in America were formerly referred to as 'savages' in order to blunt the poignancy of the atrocities being committed against them. Fast forward to the present attitude of the Israelis towards the Palestinians in the West Bank and in Gaza.

17. **The Wikipedia:** For my earlier information about John Nelson Darby and the Plymouth Brethren, I have relied heavily on the Wikipedia. Also, about the Balfour Declaration and the information about the Rothschild family, and certain other miscellaneous information I have relied on the Wikipedia.

B) Encyclopaedias :

18. *The New Encyclopaedia Britannica,* 15th Edition, updated 1997: Encyclopedia Britannica Inc., Chicago etc. I have cross-checked from this authority facts about the Plymouth Brethren, the Rothschild family, the Balfour Declaration, Britain's mandate in Palestine, the formation of the State of Israel, and last but not least, the veracity of the Ten Lost Tribes of Israel. I could not get detailed information about J. N. Darby from the ***Encyclopaedia,*** and so have had to rely heavily on the Wikipedia for the same.

The detailed references in *The New Encyclopaedia Britannica* are as follows:

a) The Lost Ten Tribes of Israel: Vol.11, pp. 627-628.

b) The Rothschild Family of Bankers: Vol. 10, pp. 201-202.

c) Israel: Vol. 22, pp. 134-147.

19. ***The Lexicon Universal Encyclopedia,*** 1989. Lexicon Publications Inc., New York. "History of Modern Israel," Vol 11, pp. 301-306.

20. ***The Lexicon Universal Encyclopedia***, 1989. Lexicon Publications Inc., New York. "Palestine," Vol. 15, pp.43-46.

C) Books :

21. : **John Hagee,** *In Defense of Israel***.** Word of Christ Ministries, Chennai, India, 2007, First Indian Edition, 2013, pp.240.

22. **John F. Walvoord.** *Major Bible Prophecies (37 crucial prophecies that affect you today*). Harper Paperbacks, Zondervan Publishing House, 1991, 544 pp.

23. **J. Dwight Pentecost**. *Things to Come (A study of Biblical Eschatology)*. O.M. Books, Secunderabad, 1999. Originally published by Zondervan Publishing House, USA, 1981, 631 pp.

24. **Elias Chacour, with Mary E.. Jensen.** *We Belong to the Land (The story of a Palestinian Israeli who* lives *for peace and reconciliation)*. Harper San Francisco, A Division of Harper Collins Publishers, 1990, 216 pp.

25. **Munther Isaac.** *The Other Side Of The Wall (A Palestinian Christian Narrative of Lament and Hope).* InterVarsity Press, USA, 2020, 248 pp.

26. **Wayne Grudem.** *Systematic Theology***.** Inter-Varsity Press, Leicester, England / Zondervan, Grand Rapids, USA, 1994, 1290 pp.

27. **Millard J. Erickson.** *Christian Theology. Second Edition*, Baker Books, Grand Rapids, Michigan, 1998, 1312 pp.

28. **William Dalrymple.** ***The Anarchy. The East India Company, Corporate Violence, and the Pillage of an Empire.*** Bloomsbury Publishing, London, 2019, 522 pp.

29. **Michael Scott-Baumann.** *The Shortest History of Israel and Palestine***.** Picador, India, 2021, 278 pp.

30. **Craig S. Keener**. *The IVP Bible Background Commentary.* ***New Testament, Second Edition,*** Inter Varsity Press Academic, 2014. 816 pp.

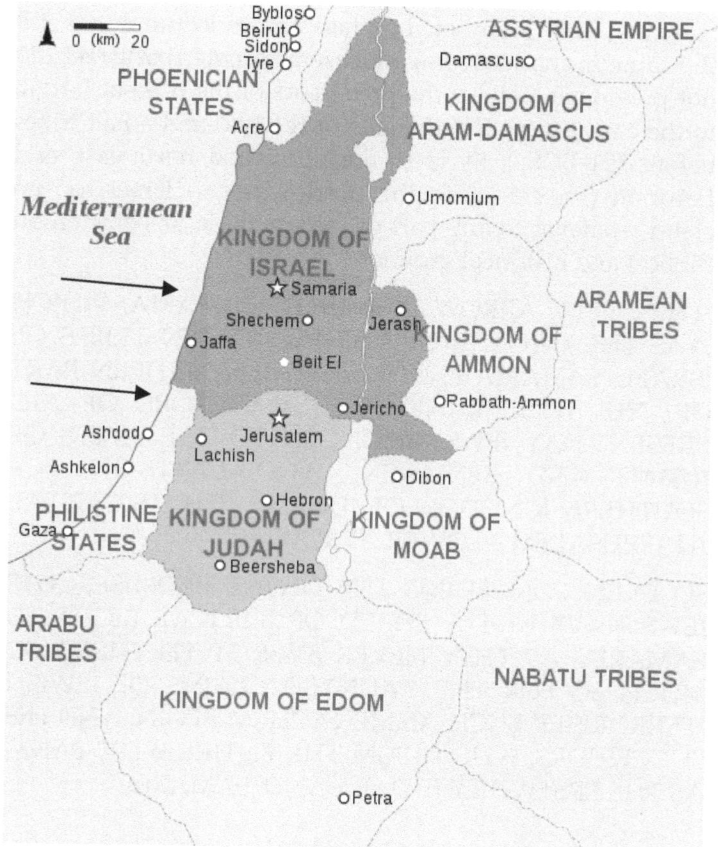

Map 'A'

The Kingdoms of Israel and Judah c. 800 BCE

This Map shows 1) the northern Kingdom of Israel (ten tribes, with Ephraim and west Manasseh occupied the area around Samaria), and 2) the southern Kingdom of Judah (two tribes—Judah and Benjamin) c. 800 BCE. Note that Samaria, the capital of Israel is to the north of Jerusalem, which was the capital of Judah. [So, as stated by the author, the ancestors of the present Jews who belonged to the two southern tribes of Judah and Benjamin, did not ever live in Samaria. So the present Jews have no claim at all to Biblical

Samaria.] N.B. Many of the place names in Judah are still the same in modern Israel. Please also note that Israel did not previously occupy the precursors of the present Jordan to the east (except for the area of the two-and-a-half tribes before 721 BCE), Syria to the north and north-east, and Lebanon (Phoenicia) to the north-west. So Israel has no claim whatever to any part of Jordan, Syria or Lebanon on Biblical and historical grounds.

THE UPPER ARROW POINTS TO SAMARIA, WHICH WAS THE CAPITAL OF THE "LOST" TEN TRIBES OF ISRAEL. SAMARIA IS NOW IN THE NORTHERN PART OF THE WEST BANK. THE ANCESTORS OF ALL PRESENT-DAY JEWS BELONGED TO THE TRIBES OF JUDAH AND BENJAMIN, WHO LIVED IN THE SOUTHERN KINGDOM OF JUDAH WITH ITS CAPITAL AT JERUSALEM – LOWER ARROW.

SO EVEN CONCEDING THE DIVINE PROMISES, THE JEWS HAVE NOT A SHRED OF BIBLICAL RIGHT TO SAMARIA, AS THEY NEVER EVER LIVED THERE. SO MUCH SO FOR THE VAUNTED CLAIMS OF JEWISH 'TERRORISTS' SUCH AS MENACHEM BEGIN, AND HIS SUCCESSORS, WHO CLAIM THE ENTIRE WEST BANK, AS THE ERSTWHILE JUDAEA AND 'SAMARIA.'

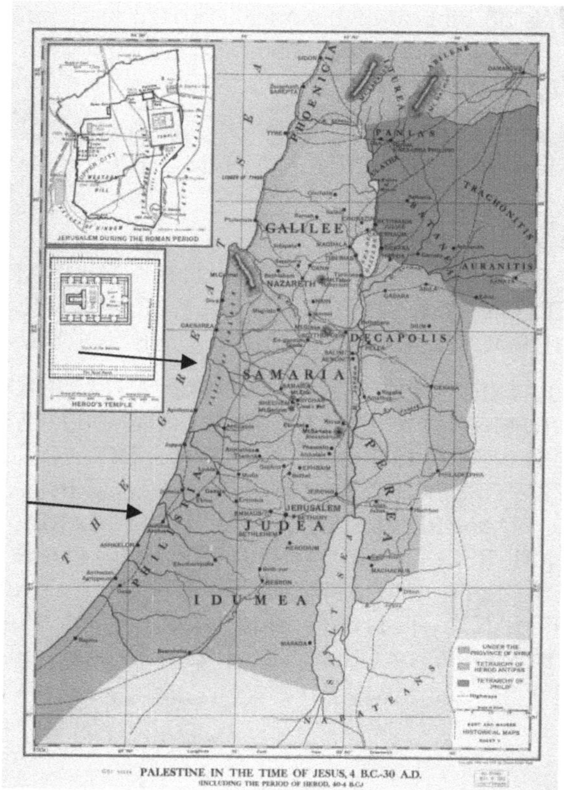

Map 'B'

Palestine towards the end of Christ's earthly ministry, c. 30 CE.

It can be seen that Palestine consisted from north to south, of the provinces of Galilee, Samaria, Judaea and Idumaea, on the extreme south. East of the Jordan were the Greek-speaking Ten Towns of the Decapolis in the north, and the province of Perea was in the south. This area east of the Jordan was formerly inhabited by the tribes of Reuben, Gad and east Manasseh before the exile of 721 BCE.

At Christ's time, in all of this area, the Jewish nation occupied only the two provinces of Judaea and Galilee. So

Israel has no Biblical or historical warrant to claim even 1 per cent more land than the 56 per cent land awarded to Israel by the UN in 1947.

(THE UPPER ARROW POINTS TO SAMARIA, AND THE LOWER ARROW TO JERUSALEM IN CHRIST'S TIME).

RECAPITULATION.

GALILEE IS TO THE NORTH OF THE UPPER ARROW. IN CHRIST'S TIME, THE JEWS ONLY LIVED IN JUDAEA TO THE SOUTH, AND GALILEE TO THE NORTH.

THE DISTRICTS OR STATES OF SAMARIA, IDUMAEA TO THE SOUTH OF JUDAEA, AND WEST OF THE DEAD SEA DID NOT BELONG TO THE JEWS. DECAPOLIS, OR THE TEN GREEK-SPEAKING TOWNS TO THE EAST OF THE JORDAN RIVER, AND EAST OF SAMARIA, ALSO DID NOT BELONG TO THE JEWS. DECAPOLIS IS IN PRESENT-DAY JORDAN. ISRAEL HAS NO CLAIM AT ALL TO ANY OF THESE TERRITORIES ON BIBLICAL AND HISTORICAL GROUNDS (PLEASE ALSO SEE MY COMMENT FOR MAP ' A').

Map 'C'

Israel and occupied Palestine today (2025 CE)

Note that in the extreme south, Israel has taken over the territory of Biblical Edom (where the descendants of Esau—Jacob's brother—used to live even in Christ's time. Edom is referred to as Idumea, and is to the south of Judea in Map 'B.') The Palestinian Arabs, who are the descendants of the Edomites, have a greater right to that area, on Biblical and historical grounds.

[Israel has not vacated the occupied lands since 58 years, in spite of numerous UN resolutions. How long must America keep stooping down lower and lower ethically and morally in its blind support to Israel, and reveal its partisanship and double standards? How are the mighty fallen! (2 Sam. 1: 19b, RSV). Note, that when Saddam Hussein took over part of Kuwait, America and the Coalition evicted Iraq in double-quick time from 1990 to early 1991. Moreover, India took over parts of Pakistan adjacent to Ferozepur in 1965, but had to return it within six months, under the Tashkent Accord.]

[The author of this book had the privilege of visiting that part of Pakistan (adjacent to Ferozepur in India): in a village called Hodiara, as a boy in December 1965, while it was still in Indian hands. He remembers seeing the Indian army soldiers entrenched in their small, concrete shelters called 'pill boxes.' This visit was possible because the author's father, the Late Dr. V.M. Mani, saw active service as an army surgeon in Ferozepur, Punjab, during the Indo-Pakistan War of August-September 1965. At that time, we had an outstanding and very upright, secular and democratic Prime Minister, Shree Lal Bahadur Shastri (who was physically diminutive versus the much taller and bigger Field Marshal Ayub Khan of Pakistan).(Previously, under the Nehru cabinet, as Railway Minister, Shastriji was so very conscientious as to voluntarily resign from the Ministry immediately after a railway accident. Moreover, even as Minister, Shastriji sent his children to school by 'tonga' or horse-cart, rather than by the official motor-car). The same Shastriji led us to victory in 1965 in spite of the alleged boast of Ayub Khan that he was looking forward to having dinner at Ashoka Hotel, which was at that time, the premier hotel in New Delhi. Ayub Khan was banking on an easy victory, on account of their recently-acquired Sabre jets and Patton tanks from USA, but these proved ineffective against the Indian Air Force and Army.

I have myself seen many captured Patton tanks at Patton Nagar during my same visit to Ferozepur in December 1965. Moreover, the two Anglo-Indian Keelor brothers (Air Marshal, Denzil and Wing Commander, Trevor) did my school, La Martiniere College, Lucknow, proud, as they both came out with flying colours during the same War, while serving in the Indian Air Force. They both shot down brand-new Pakistani Sabre jets (with their older and smaller 'Gnat' aircraft) which proved to be a turning point in the War (details now taken from the Internet, but corroborated from memory).

N.B. Dear Reader, I am not at all endorsing or glorifying War, or any form of killing, as I follow the Prince of Peace, Jesus Christ, at whose birth, the angels sang:

" Glory to God in the highest, and on earth peace, good will toward men" (Luke 2: 14, KJV).

Even though I consider myself a patriotic Indian, yet, I also consider myself to be a wider citizen of this 'global village' called the World. Hence, my intention is not to glorify the downing of the Pakistani Sabre jets by the Keelor brothers in 1965, but I am just stating it as a fact of the war. The two brothers were highly decorated by the Government of India with the 'Vir Chakra' (or Gallantry Award). However, we should not be unmindful of the loss of lives on both sides, in any war : in this case, many Indian and Pakistani lives were lost, and that is very regrettable indeed! So when I say that "the Keelor brothers did our school proud (and also St. Francis College, Lucknow, where the two brothers did most of their earlier education"), I am only referring to one side of the equation.

Diplomacy should always be the first and last option in disputes between nations, and they should stringently avoid putting matters to the '*arbitrement of the sword.*' However, a total cessation of war may not be possible in this world (as History teaches us), until Christ's Second Coming in the unknown future.

It was very unfortunate, and to India's irretrievable loss that Shastriji, on whom great hopes were pinned by our country, suddenly died in Tashkent, after signing the Peace Agreement with Ayub Khan in January 1966. It is noteworthy that one of the widest arterial roads in my home town of Kottayam, Kerala, is named Shastri road, in his honour and memory.]

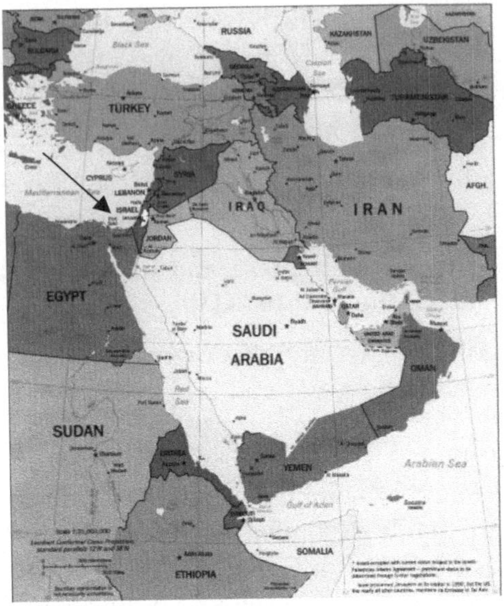

Map 'D'

The Middle East today, in 2025.

Note that Israel and Palestine are like a dot (to the left of centre in this map) in the vast panorama of the Middle East (SEE ARROW). In other words, Israel is like a 'needle in a haystack.' However, this is no ordinary needle; this 'needle' would like to dominate the haystack, not only in Palestine, but in the entire vast panorama of the Middle East. The Jewish immigrants came as sojourners to Palestine after 1922 (in order to have a homeland) but very soon they, the sojourners, became the judges (Genesis 19 : 9, RSV). The nations surrounding Israel should be doubly on their guard in order to ward off Israel's expansionistic and hegemonic tendencies, and which is a State that has no regard whatsoever for international law, or even for a modicum of justice, conscience or ethics. Israel continues to act brazenly with such impunity because of very strong diplomatic and military support from USA, whose Congress and Government are under the control of the American-Israeli

Public Affairs Committee (AIPAC), which is funded by extremely rich financiers of World Jewry. Because of this rampant favouritism by America the poor, dispossessed Palestinians have continued to get a very 'raw deal' since over one hundred years. How are the mighty fallen! (2 Sam. 1: 19b, RSV).

I would again state that great hopes are pinned on an imaginary 'Global Action Committee' without Israel and America to right the wrong! Christians and people of other faiths should pray daily to God on high: "Lord, Remember the Palestinians of Gaza and the West Bank! "

WE NEED TO CALL ON GOD ALMIGHTY TO RIGHT THIS GREAT WRONG, AS THE OTHER POWERFUL NATIONS OF THE WORLD ARE HIGH ON RHETORIC, BUT VERY COMPROMISING IN THEIR ACTIONS !

The present State of Israel has outdone the most evil kings of Israel and Judah in the Old Testament period. It is being artificially propped up by America, and the numerous Christian Zionists all over the world, but most notably in America and the UK. I consider that these countries and people are all acting against the tenets of the Bible (both Old and New Testaments). They are also acting directly against God Himself, whatever may be their pretensions!